Perspectives In Christian Education

Focus On Parent & Student Relationships

Dan L. Burrell, Ed.D – Philip C. Johnson, Ph.D – Paul Tatham, M.S.

WinePress Publishing
MUKILTEO, WA 98275

Perspectives in Christian Education
"Focus on Parent and Student Relationships"
Copyright © 1997 by Dan L. Burrell, Philip C. Johnson,
Paul Tatham

Published by:
Winepress Publishing
PO Box 1406
Mukilteo, WA 98275

Cover by **DENHAM**DESIGN, Everett, WA

Unless otherwise indicated, all scriptures are quoted from the King James Version of the Bible.

Printed in the United States of America

ISBN 1-57921-049-X
Library of Congress Catalog Card Number: 97-61498

CONTENTS

Preface v

1. Screening Problem Parents 7
Dan L. Burrell

2. Classroom Atmosphere: Creating Something with
Which You Can Live 19
Philip C. Johnson

3. Building Better Bonds between Students and
Teachers 33
Paul Tatham

4. Reaching Families through the Christian School . . . 57
Dan L. Burrell

5. Student Motivation 73
Philip C. Johnson

6. Climate Control: Creating a Class that Minimizes
Misbehavior 87
Paul Tatham

iii

7. Developing a Student Leadership Strategy 107
Dan L. Burrell

8. Parent-Teacher Conferences 119
Philip C. Johnson

9. Winning Parents through Involvement 131
Paul Tatham

10. Developing a Spiritual Restoration Program 151
Dan L. Burrell

PREFACE

"May we never forget that our calling is more spiritual than academic, more ministry than vocation, more eternal than temporal."

—**Dan L. Burrell, Ed.D.**

The Christian education movement has come of age. From its humble beginnings among mainline Protestant churches in the first half of this century, through the rapid expansion fueled by the reaction of evangelicals and fundamentalists to negative court rulings during the 60s, 70s and early 80s, to the "sorting-out period" of the last decade, Christian education has continued to change, adapt and mature. The last thirty years have seen an explosion in the quantity and quality of Christian schools. During the late 1970s and early 1980s, it was widely reported that Christian schools were starting at the rate of one every eight hours. Christian curriculum publishers, most notably A Beka Books and Accelerated Christian Education, assisted local churches and boards in establishing schools complete with training for staff and detailed curriculum.

Today, the movement is more stable and less reactionary. Teachers and administrators now have a generation of experience and, in ever-increasing numbers, advanced degrees. Our schools are as diverse as our nation. Large, multi-faceted schools serving thousands of students can be found in the same city as small, specialty schools that may serve only a score of students. Our graduates are gaining recognition for their excellence and character.

Yet, from time to time a reminder should be given as to the discipline of our philosophy, the objectives of our heritage and the outcomes we can expect to see in our future. Not every Christian school teaches a biblical worldview. Some "Christian" schools appear to be philosophically adrift and have largely become religious prep schools with a flavor that is far more *private* than *spiritual*. Educational choice, outcome-based education, Goals 2000 and other initiatives will require Christian schools that wish to remain relevant to examine their foundation and their goals.

With those thoughts in mind, the authors and the leadership of the Florida Association of Christian Colleges and Schools offers this first effort in a series, to provide a handbook of sorts to the experienced and novice educators who serve in Christian schools. It is important that we maintain a Christian perspective, an appreciation for our heritage as a movement and a focus on our endeavor. You will not agree with every suggestion in every chapter. However, it is the desire of the authors to provoke your thought, challenge your goals and encourage your mission as we lead Christian education into the next millennium. May we never forget that our calling is more spiritual than academic, more ministry than vocation, more eternal than temporal. We hope that these chapters will motivate you to a new level of excellence and ministry in your work in Christian education.

CHAPTER ONE

SCREENING PROBLEM PARENTS

"The most crucial components of screening must include prayer, wisdom and spiritual discernment."
—**Dan L. Burrell, Ed.D.**

Few things can make an admissions director's day more, than a positive interview with a family who is active in a sound Bible-preaching church and who desire to put their fresh-faced and respectful offspring into a wholesome educational environment where they will be nurtured in the admonition of the Lord. However, reality quickly sets in when the next interview of the morning is with a sullen adolescent who is sporting the latest "do" and is equipped with a variety of rings, chains and studs displayed in the most unique, not to mention uncomfortable, way. With perspiration forming on his upper lip, the interviewer feels the pressure of accurately explaining the philosophy and environment of the Christian school while desiring to sense some flicker of interest in the eyes of the prospective honor student/detention king that would indicate that he can be reached with the gospel and goals of the school.

The responsibility of screening and selecting students for your school is essential to your ministry. We have all experienced how one rebellious student can affect an entire class. Yet we also have seen what the miracle of salvation can do for an insolent spirit. Striking the balance between protecting the environment of the school and reaching out to those who are still "under construction" requires a great deal of discernment. Not every family who applies for entrance into a Christian school does so with the right motivation. We shouldn't accept every student who has parents that simply state that they are seeking a "Christian" environment. Nor can we coldly send elsewhere every student that just doesn't impress us with their grasp of Scripture and passion for world evangelism. A wise admissions director learns how to screen and what questions to ask, because there are several reasons for wanting a child in a Christian school that may spell trouble ahead.

Reason # 1: Trouble at the previous school

Many view Christian schools as "reform" institutions or schools of "last resort." While there are several fine Christian institutions that exist to salvage troubled young people (usually teens), the average Christian school is not equipped to handle most students who have experienced substantial disciplinary problems in previous schools. Severe behavioral difficulties in young children are often related to the parental philosophy of discipline in the home and sometimes (though not as often as diagnosed) the existence of emotional or behavioral disorders. As the child enters adolescence, teenage rebellion, spiritual problems and other factors come into play.

Reason # 2: Severe academic extremes

It is important for the school administration to determine the range of academic or intellectual deviations the school is prepared and equipped to serve. It is dishonest to accept a student with severe learning disabilities if the school does not have a course of study or program developed and equipped to service that child. A school with no gifted program should be absolutely candid when explaining the course offerings to an academic high-achiever. A qualified tester should be on site to assist with student assessments.

Reason # 3: "Problems" with the previous school

This reason is sometimes valid. A discerning administrator should try to ascertain the nature of problems that may have existed at the previous school or with previous teachers or administrators. I have learned to be very wary of the parent who enters an admissions interview with a long list of grievances against teachers "who are out to get" their child or have "unfair" policies, etc. I know many, if not most, of the other Christian educators in our community and they have earned my trust. Hopefully, a relationship can exist between you and the other providers of Christian education in your community (and even those in the public sector) that qualifies them to the "benefit of the doubt" and at least a courtesy call to learn their side of the story. Many of the Christian schools in our community have an informal pact that "we won't believe everything that a disgruntled parents says about your school, if you won't believe everything that the disgruntled parent says about our school." While it may be titillating to hear of the "unjust" practices of the school across town, a little research may reveal that the "injustice" would have been just as real at your school.

One of the most effective ways to screen potential problem parents is to develop a screening instrument that can be given via a questionnaire or an interview. This can be done casually or formally, though I generally find that a casual interview containing a few key questions generally gives me the information I need.

Here are some questions you may want to ask prospective parents who are applying for admission of their students to your school:

1) "Can you please provide me with the names and phone numbers of your child's most recent teacher(s) and principal?"

I have found that reticence to do so or an "explanation" of the negative responses you are likely to receive generally does not bode well for a good future relationship. Again, having a friendly relationship with other administrators helps provide discernment to responses.

2) If they are transferring from another Christian or private school: "May I call the business administrator of your previous school to make sure that your bill is current and to ask for a financial recommendation?"

If I can slip into *editorial* mode for just a moment, I think it is unethical and dishonest for Christian-school administrators to knowingly accept students into their schools who have an outstanding balance at their previous school. Many families play games with schools, accruing substantial financial obligations and then withdrawing their children rather than paying the bill. When we accept families who owe others, we are facilitating their sin and we can expect that they will do the same thing to us in the future. I would encourage the business administrators of area schools to make a pact wherein they agree not to accept students who have not made their bill current upon applying at your school and/or withdrawing from theirs. A unified front in this area will provide accountability and professionalism in our finances and will ultimately train parents in issues of honesty and integrity.

3) Ask the students: "Why do you want to attend our school?"

I have even been known to ask the student privately, "Do you really want to go to school here?" Particularly by the time a student reaches secondary school, if he or she does not want to attend your school, you can anticipate substantial trouble down the road in many cases. Often through the posture and demeanor of the student during the interview, I can tell whether or not they are applying because they recognize a need in their life and want to go to a Christian school or if this is a case where the parents are requiring the student to go to a Christian school. There have been some instances in which I have made exceptions and allowed a non-cooperative student admission in the hope that he would experience a change of heart, but I must confess that the success stories have been rather limited.

4) Ask the student about behavior that will bring them into conflict with the school's conduct code.

If your school has a policy against the use of tobacco, find out if the student smokes. If you have a policy against rock music, find out who the student's favorite musicians are. There are going to be conflicts in any school-student relationship. It is a good idea to try and determine the potential for future conflicts and over what issues they may erupt.

5) Specifically ask, "Have you ever been suspended or expelled from school?"

In our school district, a student who manages to be suspended or expelled from public school is...shall we say...*significantly* behaviorally challenged? Chances are, if we admit them into our student body, we can anticipate the addition of several new rules in the student handbook that we had never even *considered* before. Beware that it is not uncommon for parents and students to lie about this, and a phone call to the previous dean of discipline generally exposes the sins of the past. We also have a policy that addresses this problem: Misrepresentations made to gain entrance into the school, upon coming to light, will result in immediate dismissal.

6) "Are you involved or have you ever been involved in any legal action against a school or school employee?"

Considering the litigious nature of our culture, it is a good idea to ascertain early into the relationship what the potential for depositions and court dates might be.

Here are some other recommendations you might want to consider to assist you with screening your students:

1. Request reference forms from at least three people who know the student including their pastor/Sunday school teacher, a former teacher or school administrator, and a non-family member who has known the student for at least one year.
2. Require the student to write a paragraph or page detailing why they want to attend your school.
3. Have the student complete an "interest inventory" which should give you some insight into their personal world.

The following are some sample items you could put on such an inventory:

- What do you do on a typical Sunday?
- If you had a free hour, how would you spend it?
- What is your favorite TV show?
- Who is your favorite entertainer?
- What is your favorite verse from the Scriptures?
- What do you want to be doing in 10 years?
- If you died today, where would you go? Why did you answer in the way you did?
- What is the last good book that you have read?
- Describe your relationship with your parents.
- Whose choice is it for you to go to a Christian school?
- What percentage of your friends uses tobacco? Alcohol?

4. Be very specific about your expectations for your stdents. Make sure that they understand the homework load, code of conduct, the uniform or dress code, limitations on outside activities, etc.
5. Consider the use of a *probationary* period. This allows time for observation and provides an "escape hatch" should the student demonstrate this wasn't a good choice.
6. Consider a separate, private interview with older students. During this type of interview, many students will be more comfortable opening up with their fears, questions and hesitations.
7. Have a standard for evaluation. Occasionally we feel pressured to make entrance exceptions for a student who can infect others with a poor attitude. By having an ad-

missions committee review applications or by having some sort of entrance policy, the temptation to lower the bar on entrance requirements is diminished.

Now, personally, this chapter has been far too negative for my taste. So let me end it with some positive suggestions for attracting the *right* kind of families to your school ministry.

Utilize personal contacts

The number one most effective way to advertise your school is *word of mouth*. There is no more effective advertisement than a satisfied customer. Encourage your current, satisfied families to recommend potential new students to your school. We have even encouraged our families to recruit by offering a credit to their account for each student that they recommend who enrolls in our school.

Put your students on display in good churches

Form a performance choir or a drama or puppet team that can visit local churches and minister. This is great training for your students and a great testimony for your school.

Emphasize the positives

Traditional academics, family values, firm-but-loving discipline, high academic standards, values instruction, etc., are terms that communicate your philosophy clearly and which may help you attract those who desire those characteristics for their child's learning environment.

Celebrate excellence

People are willing to pay a price if they know they will receive a superior product. By developing a program that elevates character, produces high academics, has a clean, neat learning environment, contains poised, articulate students and professional and balanced teachers, you will earn a reputation for excellence. If the Christian school is not committed to excellence, from whom can we expect it?

Toot your horn

Not in an arrogant or prideful way, but in a way that gives honor to whom honor is due. As your students achieve, issue press releases. Give the parents of students who perform well a bumper sticker for their car. Utilize the marquis on the front of your school to recognize desired accomplishment. Encourage what you expect to produce.

Advertise in the right places

If you are going to spend money on advertising (keeping in mind that the *most* effective and least costly advertising is word of mouth), spend it wisely. Look for where your market will be reading. Advertise on Christian radio or near churches, place an ad in the Christian directories, purchase a mailing list of people who would share a similar (usually conservative) philosophy of life. Don't waste money on blitz advertising. Our school once accidentally sent a brochure for our school to a retirement complex that contained over 20,000 people over the age of 55. Does anyone want to guess how many students we enrolled out of that development?

The most important aspect of screening families for entrance into your school is found in James 1:5, "If any of you lack wisdom, let him ask of God, that giveth to all men liberally, and upbraideth not, and it shall be given him." No screening instrument or policy will catch every problem. There will be times when an exception can and should be made and a life will be salvaged. The most crucial components of screening must include prayer, wisdom and spiritual discernment.

We can never afford to forget that our mission is primarily a *spiritual* mission—not just an academic mission. If we train the mind and neglect the soul, we will have educated fools who have information without character. Let us bathe our enrollment process in prayer, and may we seek the guidance of the Holy Spirit in every entrance decision.

CHAPTER TWO

CLASSROOM ATMOSPHERE: CREATING SOMETHING WITH WHICH YOU CAN LIVE

"The main aim of all teachers ought to be to provide an atmosphere in the classroom that allows students to feel secure, promotes academic learning and encourages spiritual growth."

—Philip C. Johnson, Ph.D.

I was twenty-two years old. I had just graduated from college and was freshly married. I was also starting my very first teaching job with all of the innocence of any idiot just about ready to enter into battle with only a pencil behind his ear. My first class consisted of 31 fifth-graders. At first glance they seemed harmless enough. On the first day of school they appeared quiet and quite eager to absorb my vast and boundless wisdom. They were veritable sponges just ready to soak up what I had to offer. Boy, was I naive. By the fourth day, these sweet, desk-bound students were everywhere except in their desks. Inside the first week of my career, I had inadvertently created a classroom atmosphere, with which I knew I could *not* live. I had to do something, and I had to do it fast.

Every classroom has some kind of atmosphere—some kind of ambiance. It might be an atmosphere somewhat akin to a Nazi prison camp or maybe even something like a three-ring circus, but believe me, there *is* atmosphere. The proper atmosphere, however, doesn't just happen. It has to be carefully developed and cultivated. If the teacher does not take an active role in creating the atmosphere he or she desires, the students *will* create the atmosphere that they think they want. Someone will take charge of setting the mood in your class; it had better be you. Atmosphere is more than just the right lighting and music. Its essence comes from *you*. Let's examine some of the different classroom styles and personalities that create them.

Different Styles: Same Goals

Just as there are many different types of personalities, there will also be different types of classroom atmospheres. Different people have different styles and different tolerance levels. Classrooms should be different and should reflect the *je ne sais quois* of the individual. There is no reason for each class to be a carbon copy of every other class. This is not feasible nor is it desirable. The one thing that *should* remain constant from class to class is an atmosphere that promotes the overall goals of Christian education. The main aim of all teachers ought to be to provide an atmosphere in the classroom that promotes security, academic learning and spiritual growth.

Here are some of the most common classroom styles of teachers:

The quiet classroom

In this type of classroom you can hear a pin drop. More importantly, you can hear the fire alarm. The teacher herself is usually very soft-spoken. This kind of classroom makes it very easy for the teacher to communicate without interruption. Personally, I love the quiet classroom. It holds the potential for great educational success. But it is important to remember that students who are sleeping or enjoying a mid-afternoon coma are also very quiet. Quietness does not always mean that we have the students' attention. It just means that they are *quiet*.

The relaxed classroom

This classroom is run by Mr. Joe Comfortable. Surely you know Joe. He's the one who keeps an extra pair of slippers in his cabinet and a nice fluffy pillow in his desk drawer. There is usually clutter on the floor and feet up on the desks. Everyone is cozy and students feel right at home. The problem is, they're not at home; they're at school. Students ought to feel comfortable in their classroom, but not as comfortable as they would feel in their bathrobes. School is the students' place of business. As the classroom reflects this, so does student behavior, attitudes, work habits and success.

The loud classroom

Often the teacher of the loud class is the last to even realize it. If this is not your class, then it is invariably next door to you. This teacher and their class go on their merry, clamorous way through the day and through the hallways disturbing others and are blissfully ignorant of it. In this type of classroom, while everyone may be awake, no one ever hears all that the teacher in trying to communicate. The competition for attention is too intense and the teacher spends a great deal of time repeating what only needed to be said once.

The party classroom

You might as well bring your own chips and soft drinks to this class. This is the fun and exciting class, at least on

23

the surface. The teacher of this type of classroom is often viewed as very popular by the students and seen as very irritating to the administration. The party classroom always has something to celebrate. The major concern associated with this class is whether or not the students will learn enough to one day celebrate their own graduation.

The restrictive classroom

Welcome to prison camp. Often motivated by fear, this teacher is so preoccupied with all that *might* go wrong that he keeps the reigns too tight. Discipline is misunderstood and is replaced by oppression. This class is certainly not going to get out of hand very often, but they're not going to have any fun either. This atmosphere will crush spirits and stifle creativity. One of two things will happen in this type of classroom: Either the students will become terribly bitter and apathetic, or the prisoners will revolt. Either way it won't be attractive.

The out-of-control classroom

Enter at your own risk. Anything goes in this class. Lots of noise is the soundtrack, and chaos and confusion are the stars of this production. This scenario provides no security for anyone, especially the teacher. Many precious hours of prime educational time are forever lost because of the lack of control.

Finding the Balance

Every type of classroom and teacher personality comes with positives and negatives. The challenge is to become balanced and learn how to maximize one's strength and minimize one's weaknesses. Remember, the objective is to produce a balanced class and a class that will make steady progress without driving its teacher and those around you toward the brink of a nervous breakdown.

So, how does a teacher manage to transcend their own personal style and develop a classroom atmosphere that will yield the right kind of students? Here are some general principles that apply to everyone, regardless of personal style.

Make simple, comprehensive rules

Don't complicate things. Make rules that will be easy to understand and follow. When rules are clear and students understand their responsibilities, they will feel more secure. Security is something that students crave. They *want* to know their boundaries. Of course, wanting to know those boundaries and testing you up to the limit of said boundaries is quite another story. I am reminded of a trip where I took a group of eighth grade students to Washington, DC. While waiting for a bus, I clearly explained where I wanted the students to wait. In the interest of safety and knowing how parents frown upon having their children run over by busses, I told them that they were not to cross a certain line on the sidewalk. There was plenty of room for them to romp and frolic behind the line, but that would not do for my students. Each and every one of them, clearly in violation of the international laws of personal body space, were standing as close to one another and this arbitrary line as possible. I had brought them 700 miles away from home and they still wanted to get as close to the "line" as possible. Even though the students were pushing the limits, they knew the boundary, they knew the consequences of crossing it, and they did not cross it. That works for me.

It is also wise to make the rules you give comprehensive. Instead of telling students that there will be no note passing, whispering, talking, giggling, turning around and glancing sideways at other students, just tell them that there will be no *communicating* during class time without permission. That is a whole lot easier to remember and easier for you to enforce. Likewise, if you tell students that they need to keep their hands to themselves at all times, you won't have Billy whining that you said not to hit anyone, but you never said anything about *pinching* or *poking*.

Set the tone from the first day

Don't wait. Don't assume that if the students are compliant on the first day that they will stay that way. That is a time-honored ploy used by clever students to trap innocent teachers. Don't fall for it! What you want and what you expect for the school year must be clearly explained as if you expect the very worst to happen. We seem to have no trouble preparing quite carefully for the possibility of a fire or tornado. We relate the procedures and practice the operation so that there will be no misunderstanding in case of an emergency. Likewise, we should clearly relate to students what is expected of them and what we will and will not tolerate in the classroom. This *must* be done within the first few days. I cannot stress this strongly enough: With students, there is no grace period. They spend the entire first week testing you for weaknesses, and they are quite good at detecting our vulnerabilities. Be forewarned: They will use this gathered information against you.

Be consistent

Consistency is one of the rarest virtues around these days. It is also one of the most difficult qualities to acquire but one of the most important qualities to develop in order to be successful in setting the classroom atmosphere you desire. A consistent, dependable classroom atmosphere depends greatly on your ability to be consistent in your own emotions, attitudes and application of the rules. This requires real maturity and dependency upon God to maintain mastery over your emotions.

Have a sense of fun

After you have established who is in charge in your classroom (and for those of you who have just tuned in, that answer is *you*), you can set up a very enjoyable classroom inside the order you have created. This is what balance is all about. The necessary rigidity and structure of a planned and fruitful day can be effectively punctuated by laughter, variety, excitement and a healthy appreciation for the ridiculous that often surrounds us. For the teacher who has implemented the previously mentioned safeguards, all of this can occur without anyone getting out of control.

The Ingredients Of A Desirable Classroom

Just as in any good recipe, there are several ingredients crucial for any class to possess. Here are four that I have found to be indispensable.

Sense of calm

A sense of calm implies that the teacher is in confident control. How pleasant it is for students to come into a class where there is order and preparedness. Students feel a sense of peace and are then able to concentrate on the work at hand.

Sense of quietness

Quietness is not synonymous with boredom. The kind of quietness that is desirable is the type that allows for instruction. The teacher should never have to compete for the class's attention. The students should never have to miss valuable information because a teacher permits too much noise. Set your classroom "noise-o-meter" carefully, for it will be difficult to reset later in the year. Most teachers will have trouble keeping things at the line they've drawn; it will be nearly impossible to move the line further back.

Sense of expectation

Hushed excitement. Anticipation. Having a sense of purpose. All of these are part of the indispensable atmosphere of the superior classroom. Students need to feel and know that each day, each class and each moment of the class is vital to their future. This type of atmosphere causes students to come to class with homework assignments completed, pencils sharpened and minds ready. If students come to your class totally unprepared time and time again, perhaps it is time to ask yourself if you've failed to create the atmosphere of *expectation*.

Sense of security

Kids need to feel safe. We all want to feel safe. *I* want to feel safe! I want to know what to expect. I absolutely love variety; but like most people, I like it inside the security of the predictable. It's like the cream filling in a Hostess cupcake. Certainly we can all appreciate the consistency of the delicious devil's-food cake and chocolate icing. We've come to feel comfortable with it; it's very reassuring. But then you bite into that cream filling and, "WOW!" It's like a little surprise, a breath of fresh air, a sugar rush, all wrapped up in the familiar and predictable. Ah, the blessings of well-planned, spontaneous, predictable variety!

Students want to know what to expect from you and from the class. If you are prone to mood swings, students are never going to know how to prepare for you. They never know whether you will let them get away with something one day and crack down on them the next. More importantly, they won't know what you expect from them regarding assignments. You can and should set your academic standards high; just let students feel that you are consistent and that your expectations are consistent. Also, regardless of the difficulty of the task at hand, students need to feel secure in their relationship to you. It is emotionally exhausting for students to feel as if you are their buddy one day and on your black list the next. Cultivate a relationship that allows you to be their teacher and yet allows you to love them unconditionally. You will be surprised at how well your students thrive in that kind of atmosphere.

Do Looks Count?

In conclusion, let's turn our attention toward appearances. Sometimes we can get so busy with the countless other things that go on during the course of a day that we forget to pay attention to our surroundings. As superficial as it may sound, the way your classroom looks is an important contributor to the overall atmosphere. For students and others who come into your class, the appearance of your class provides the first impression and valuable information about you and your style.

Mr. Smith mentioned casually over the teacher's lunch table that he couldn't understand why his students were such slobs and so disorganized. After handing him three napkins in hopes that he would wipe the ketchup off his upper lip, I asked him to accompany me to his classroom. It was then that Mr. Smith realized a very important principle: Students mirror their teachers in all kinds of indirect ways. Mr. Smith's room was full of clutter. I could barely find his desk beneath papers that should have been graded weeks ago. The bulletin boards seemed *seasonally challenged*. But I'm one of those picky people who feel that Christmas decorations should come down sometime *before* Easter. In short, Mr. Smith's students were disorganized and sloppy because Mr. Smith was disorganized and sloppy.

Students respond to their physical environment. Here are some considerations for the physical atmosphere of your classroom:

- **Keep it clean!** Have a couple of times during the course of the day where students do a quick midday clean up. You'll be surprised how much better the room will look and how much better you'll feel.
- **Keep it organized!** Have a place for everything. Instruct students where you want their book bags, lunch boxes and coats to go. Have a specific place where you want homework to be placed. Do the same for yourself so that *your* desk looks neat and *you* can find the things that you need.
- **Change your bulletin boards!** This seems so easy in September. By May you've still got Abraham Lincoln sitting up on the board; only by now half of his leg has been torn off and someone has stapled George Washington's cherry tree to Abe's nose. Be proactive in providing bulletin boards and wall displays in your class room that provide the following: (1) educational moti-

vation, (2) seasonal congruity, (3) spiritual emphasis and (4) something to make them laugh.

- **Use music**! Many classrooms, especially homerooms, can have great Christian music playing as students enter. This is a wonderful way to put a song in their hearts, lift spirits and set students' minds on the Lord first thing in the morning.

Developing a great classroom atmosphere involves a multitude of things. It is definitely a multifaceted endeavor. In setting a proper classroom atmosphere, teachers need to desire a setting that eliminates distractions, sets a purpose and promotes excellent work habits. This type of classroom happens by design. It must be thought out well in advance, meticulously planned and carefully implemented. Who knows, if you do it well and create just the right ambiance, your classroom may become the most talked about "place to be" in town. You might even have to start taking reservations. "Will that be a table for eight…?"

CHAPTER THREE

BUILDING BETTER BONDS
BETWEEN STUDENTS
AND TEACHERS

"To most students it is the teachers who are the school. If students are ever going to bond with their school, it is largely up to the teachers themselves."

—Paul Tatham, M.S.

Nicole whimpered as her mother nudged her out the door toward the waiting school bus. She did not want to go to school. It wasn't that Nicole missed her mommy; she just plain didn't like the Christian school she attended, and especially her teacher. The class was boring and the teacher was "mean," she claimed.

Now her mother had to literally push her out the door each morning, and it had reached the point where Nicole was feigning illness in order to stay home. Exasperated, mother and daughter sat down together on the edge of Nicole's bed one evening for a mother-daughter talk. "Tell me the *real* reason you don't want to go to school, honey," implored her mother.

Nicole began to sob. "I don't know, Mommy. It's just that school is no fun. All we do is sit all day and work in those dumb workbooks. The teacher doesn't ever let us get out of our seats, and we never get to do anything special. And she's always yelling at us."

Though obviously exaggerated, mother suspected that Nicole might be telling the truth, for her junior-high son had expressed similar sentiments. Nicole, like her older brother, attended Victory Christian School; but according to them, life at Victory was anything but. Both children were growing more vocal each day about their desire to attend another school—*any* school but Victory.

Bonding Starts with Hiring

Sadly, Nicole and her brother are not alone. Their plight is not uncommon in some Christian schools. Having entered their Christian school filled with excitement and high hopes, that initial enthusiasm has now dissipated. When asked specifically who or what they don't like about their school, they most often cite their teachers. To most students it is the teachers who are the school. The administration, the facilities, and even the curriculum take a back seat when it comes to shaping a student's view of his school. If students are ever going to bond with their school, it is largely up to the teachers themselves.

It is of paramount importance, therefore, that the administration take great pains to hire teachers who can build that bond. The administrator responsible for recruiting faculty should be alert to clues as to which applicants have the ability to cultivate a student-teacher kinship. Among those clues are the following:

Does the applicant indicate a love for students?

Strangely, some in the teaching profession do not really like kids. Beside the obvious dilemma that it would be difficult to have a school without them, such an attitude begs the question of why they continue to teach. Their conversation is peppered with disparaging references to students they have had or known. They portray teaching as a chore. Once in the classroom, such teachers *do not* endear themselves to their students, for the students know intuitively which teachers love them, and they respond accordingly.

Does the applicant show warmth?

A teacher, to be most effective, must be personable. Students should gravitate to her, because her smile goes a long way in removing barriers. When interviewing the candidate, this quality should be evident, for the teacher who is cool and distant will have trouble bonding. In the 1957 Philip E. Jacob study on the influence of school on students, he found that the teachers who profoundly influence students are "likely to be persons whose own value commitments are firm and openly expressed, and who are outgoing and warm in their personal relations with students."

Is the applicant a worthy Christian role model?

A Christian teacher is far more than his lesson plans, and students will learn more from him than subject matter. The inquiring administrator is asking himself this fundamental question: "Would I want my own son or daughter to emulate this teacher?"

Students learn more from a teacher's *ways* than his *words*. Someone has said, "The teacher teaches for good or ill largely because of what he *is*. His attitudes toward God and life, his likes and dislikes, his prejudices, his very habits of speech and manner of dress are as inevitably a part of his teaching as any technical skills or methods." Not only do countless research studies bear this out, but God's Word is also clear on it. Luke 6:40 plainly states that a student will turn out like his teacher—not merely his teacher's teachings. It is interesting to note that Jesus chose His disciples to be "*with* Him" (Mark 3:14), knowing that they would learn more from *Him* than from His *words*. When the Sanhedrin, in Acts 4, saw the boldness of Peter and John, they knew "that they had been *with* Jesus." Who a student is *with* is vitally important.

Is the applicant enthusiastic?

Enthusiasm goes a long way in teaching, for the teacher who teaches "with all his might" (Ecclesiastes 9:10) has a distinct advantage over the teacher who doesn't. Do the applicant's references confirm that he has some "zip"? Does he show it over the phone or during the interview? Is there any glimmer of excitement in his eye when he talks about the classroom?

Is the applicant courteous?

By and large, students will respond courteously to the teacher who displays courtesy to them (Proverbs 18:24). Hints of civility usually surface in the interview: Does the applicant interrupt conversation? Does he demonstrate proper manners? Does the applicant talk only of himself?

Is the applicant emotionally healthy?

One clue to a person's emotional health is whether or not he has a sense of humor. In most interviews, face-to-face or over the phone, there is opportunity for a chuckle or two. If the applicant shows little sense of humor, it may be a hint of an unbalanced personality. Is the person an optimist or a pessimist? An "upper" or a "downer"? Because teaching is often a thankless task, the teacher must come equipped with a healthy endowment of optimism.

Someone easily depressed does not belong in the classroom. Although the administrator is not looking for a teacher who is naively cheerful, he is looking for someone with a positive outlook on life.

Schools are wary of applicants who carry too much emotional baggage. An applying teacher may be caught up in the turmoil of a faltering marriage, or beset with financial worries. Someone about to minister to needy students cannot himself be needy.

Bonding Is Implemented by the Teacher

Although the school atmosphere that the administration creates may encourage bonding, it is the teachers themselves who must make it happen. They are the ones on the front line, in the trenches. Be assured, teachers, that you have the earnest prayer support of the administration, but they cannot do it for you.

When we speak of bonding, we are basically talking about *rapport*. A French word that means *harmonious relationship*, rapport is that indefinable magic that unites a teacher and his class. Although intangible, it is invaluable, for the teacher possessing rapport with his students finds them sincerely *wanting* to please him. Teachers who manage to reach this blessed state find teaching to be the rewarding experience it was meant to be.

Once she has reached that point, the teacher is virtually assured of success. She is home free. A teacher with rapport can do no wrong; a teacher without it can do no right. Students taught by a teacher with strong rapport will make allowances for many of her mistakes and blunders; students taught by a teacher lacking rapport will allow her nothing.

We're all insurance salesmen

Until rapport is established, only superficial learning takes place. Sure, the students will learn geometry theorems and even be able to properly apply them to problems, but their hearts won't be in it. For that to happen, students must be won to the teacher first before they will be *really* interested in what he has to offer. Like any salesman, the teacher must sell himself before he can hope to sell his product.

An insurance salesman, stepping into your living room, seeks to build rapport first—by complimenting your wallpaper, your furniture, the family dog, or your wisdom in picking his agency. *Then* he opens his briefcase. Likewise, not until the teacher has gained a measure of rapport will the class "have ears to hear."

The integrated life

Talk of Bible integration is common conversation in Christian schools. We all understand the importance of incorporating scriptural truth into our lessons and acknowledge the assertion that without it we are nothing more than a well-disciplined public school. To overcome the human tendency to compartmentalize spiritual things, our challenge is to weave scriptural truth into the fabric of every subject. So we trade integration ideas among ourselves—on likening our resurrected bodies to that caterpillar cocoon in science class, that circle we drew on the board in math class to represent God's endless love, or God's providence in history in the defeat of the Spanish Armada. But we sometimes forget that the most potent form of Bible integration is the integrated life. At least six times the Apostle Paul said, in essence, "Follow me." How many teachers can say that to their students?

More than mere words—scriptural analogies or comparisons we make in class—it is our *lives* that shout the loudest to our kids. It's our *ways,* not our *words*, that carry the day. We can talk all we want about God's obvious hand in the design of the human immune system in biology class, but all our God-talk can be instantly erased when we resort to a terse put-down to correct a daydreaming student.

How a teacher teaches is every bit as important as *what* she teaches. Does she model Christ to her students by the patience she exhibits with that disorganized student—the one who never seems to have the proper textbook, let alone open to the right page? Is Christ manifest by the way she handles Kevin, the one who manages to lose his homework every night? Is she willing to graciously re-explain every day for a week, if necessary, a math process that the class should have grasped the first day? Will her ego allow a student's simpler explanation of nuclear fusion—an explanation that classmates find easier to grasp than the teacher's—to replace her own. When it comes to impact, students will remember their *teacher* far longer than what their teacher *taught.*

Students bond with teachers who flesh out their Christianity, and they gradually assimilate the teacher's behavior patterns as their own. When my youngest daughter was in lower elementary, I would sometimes catch her "playing school" and could tell instantly which teacher on our school staff she was mimicking. She had every gesture and voice inflection down cold.

Some of our modeling is exemplary, some isn't. The teacher lacking patience will not beget that quality in his students. The critical teacher will produce students given to gossip. The teacher who is quick to encourage will find his students so ministering to each other. The praying teacher may find some of his students huddled together in a small prayer group during lunch. For good or ill, we beget ourselves.

A Christian schoolteacher is not "being spiritual" only when he talks about the things of the Lord. Spirituality is much broader than that, encompassing *any* word or deed that nudges students closer to God. That may be something as insignificant as patting a student on the head or picking up his pencil from under his desk.

We are all in the modeling business, and students need teachers who model their Christianity well. As they observe their teacher before them each day, he portrays to them a living object lesson that reflects his Lord. As they size up their teacher, they are sizing up his Lord. What the teacher covers in his lesson plan is important, certainly, but *how* he covers it is what impacts students.

I'm not too proud to admit it

The teacher who presents himself as infallible is out of touch with reality and will rarely bond with his students. Kids, even youngsters, soon learn that their esteemed teachers occasionally blunder, and the teacher who attempts to bury his mistakes is usually a person with an anemic self-image—a person who dares not expose himself.

A teacher who cannot laugh at himself will have students who do. When he misspells a word on the overhead, for instance, then offers some questionable excuse rather than admitting his error, he is only kidding himself; no one is fooled. The person who attempts to cover his transgressions, exhorts Solomon, will not prosper (Proverbs 28:13).

When a teacher goofs publicly, he should apologize publicly. When he does something dumb, and we all do, he should admit it. Every one of us can tell of at least one class incident in which we tried pathetically to mask a mistake and maintain our dignity, while struggling to suppress giggling students who were not fooled. Transparent teachers—teachers with nothing to hide—endear themselves to their classes.

A faultless teacher is something of a joke, anyway, since everyone knows there *ain't* no such creature. Students under such an exalted ruler will make it their mission to expose his feet of clay by laying traps that make his humanity embarrassingly apparent.

Some teachers fear that by admitting a mistake they will lose the respect, and thus the control, of their class. But actually the opposite is true. Apologies usually serve to enhance a teacher's credibility and appeal.

Positively popular

A teacher who is positive has gone a long way to enhance her net worth. Students will be attracted to her. When correcting a child, for example, the wise teacher is careful to "speak the truth *in love*" (Ephesians 4:15). Instead of chiding her primary students who are not ready for dismissal, she stimulates the entire class to action with: "I like the way Evan had everything ready to go!" This has a positive ripple effect, as the rest of the class scurries to emulate Evan.

You might hear the following if you were to eavesdrop on positive teachers:

- "I think Brittany is almost ready for juice and cookies."
- "We draw on our *paper*, Brian" (not on our desk).
- "I'm putting you in this seat, Jonathan, because I think it might help you to win the prize."

- "Carmen has really studied this subject and can answer almost every question, but I'd like to know who else can answer my question."
- "It's too bad we won't be able to have popcorn today, because we wasted so much time. But perhaps we can work faster tomorrow."

Positive reinforcement, especially that offered within earshot of a student's classmates, does much to build bonds. Having students applaud for Jimmy, showing astonishment over Sherry's science project, or thanking Darren for carrying Brenda's books will all go a long way in ensuring that such behavior is repeated. Some teachers set aside *praise moments*—when students are encouraged to share what they appreciate about someone.

To be most effective, research shows, a teacher's praise should be specific, low-key and sincere. In specifically praising a student, the teacher would thank a student for raising her hand, not simply for "being good." Low-key praise is especially important at the high school level, since many students do not want to be regarded by their peers as *too* well behaved! Students in upper elementary and above easily detect insincere praise.

It's amazing how quickly we can focus on the negative. That's probably because negative student behavior draws attention to itself more than positive behavior. Therefore, we tend to concentrate on Proverbs 23:13 ("withhold not correction") to the neglect of Proverbs 3:27 ("withhold not good.")

Yuk it up

Humor has its place in the classroom, for humor is a gift from God that makes life bearable. And some days can be quite unbearable! Granted, certain ages can handle humor better than others. And sure, the teacher may have to temper himself with particular classes that tend to get carried away, but the teacher need not shun a little levity now and then. Remember: "A merry heart doeth [a class] good like a medicine" (Proverbs 17:22).

Used in moderation, humor can defuse a potentially disruptive situation. For instance: The teacher who smiles as he utters something that he knows may arouse a few snickers—perhaps a strange-sounding Amazon village—has disarmed the class. He has beaten them to the punch by showing them that he is just as humored by the name as they are. The teacher who, on the other hand, takes a this-is-serious-stuff attitude is headed into a battle he cannot win.

On some occasions, a student will come across with a truly humorous line. Presupposing that it is delivered at an appropriate time, the teacher who *leads* his class in laughter comes out the winner. To pretend that something is not funny, when it actually is, can become more humorous to the class than the joke itself.

I'm not partial!

Teachers who play favorites will have difficulty bonding with their classes. Although every human being is biased to some degree, the teacher who is dominated by them does not belong in a Christian school. "To have respect of persons is not good," warns Proverbs 28:21.

We are naturally attracted to some students more than others, but we must be careful not to make it obvious. Otherwise, it can lead to resentment and backlash from students outside our circle of favorites.

Partiality comes in many guises. Racial partiality is certainly the one most often addressed today and is endemic to all cultures of the world. Other prejudices, however, are more insidious and pervasive. Take the partiality of wealth. Wealthy people have a funny effect on us. We find ourselves playing up to them, perhaps hoping that they will adopt us! A teacher may find himself treating a student in a whole new light since learning that his father owns an island in the Bahamas!

Gender partiality has been given much press lately and is a concern of which we should be aware. Certain subjects lend themselves to this. History classes, when taught by a man, typically are taught from the great-leader viewpoint and focus on warfare as the determining shaper of our past. The boys in his class will be enthralled, while the girls wish their teacher would focus more on what people of the past wore and ate. According to the research, girls are generally perceived more favorably by teachers, so they are disciplined less harshly and graded more generously. Teachers must guard against gender partiality.

We're more aware of the bias of beauty. We live in a society in which image is everything, and physical beauty is highly prized. The media has touted it as a legitimate end in itself. But the Lord, unlike us, is completely unimpressed with the outward appearance. Following the Master's cue, a mature teacher is one who has trained himself to look instead for *inward* beauty.

Some of us suffer from the bias of intelligence. We tend to respond almost exclusively to those students who respond to us. The students who keep abreast with us during class discussions, nodding appropriately, are usually our favorites.

Watch the partiality of position. Be leery of playing favorites with the children of associates, colleagues, supervisors, neighbors and church members—people we know. It is easy to downplay the misconduct of the son or daughter of our pastor, board member or tennis partner. For this reason, principals caution their staffs against cultivating abnormally close relationships with any one family. We must remain professionally aloof, treating each student as equitably as possible. Teachers may be tempted to give certain students privileges not afforded to other students—access to themselves, their classroom, their desk. It will not go unnoticed.

The partiality of mannerisms, I would dare say, is scarcely recognized among us. Yet it exists. We may find the habits and mannerisms of some students particularly irksome, and certain things they do, though minor to most people, are major irritants to us. It may be the way the student walks, talks, combs her hair, or even sneezes, but it can overshadow everything else that student does. Just as we can blot out a million-dollar view by covering our eyes with two pennies, so we can overlook someone's good qualities because our view of them is darkened by one or two bad ones. Professionals call this weakness of human nature the *halo effect*; but whatever one calls it, we must avoid it.

Just make me look good in front of my friends

One of the most powerful ways a teacher can bond with his students has to do with peer acceptance. Those of us who teach adolescents never cease to be amazed at the lengths to which young people will go to win the approval of their peers. Although we often preach against such behavior, and we should, we must admit that those same forces likely drove us at that age.

The wise teacher, then, follows the cardinal rule to publicly uphold a student whenever feasible in the best possible light. Make a student look good in the eyes of his classmates and he will love you for it. We, therefore, avoid put-downs and sarcasm. Teachers who correct aberrant behavior with sarcasm are only challenging students to respond in kind in order to save face with their peers.

Avoid comparisons. When students compare themselves to their peers it can lead to either discouragement or arrogance. Students who play the comparison game may be inclined to cry out to God, "Why hast Thou made me thus?" (Romans 9:20). When teachers join in, little good results. "This class didn't do nearly as well on the test as my third-period class," we say. Or we sometimes exalt one sibling over another: "Your *brother* never had trouble with algebra." Students resent being contrasted with someone else, just as teachers do when students tell them, "Miss Chapin never did it that way."

Class discussions are prime opportunities for teachers to bond with their students. A student who interjects a comment or asks a question is actually going out on a limb for you. How you respond signals to him and the rest of the class how *safe* it is to cooperate with you. If we respond with sarcasm, mockery or even unappreciation, rapport begins to erode. If several students have tested the waters and found them cold, the whole class will draw back.

A student who participates in class needs the teacher's support. When he flounders in answering a question, rescue him with a face-saver such as, "You're probably thinking of…."; then supply the answer. When a student gives a wrong answer, praise him for his attempt. When a student makes a point you overlooked, commend him on his insight rather than responding with an ego-damaging, "I was coming to that." Teachers who understand the power of peer acceptance and gauge their interaction accordingly will have students who rise up to call them blessed.

Don't forget the average kid

The most overlooked student in school is the average kid. Those who constitute the extremities of the educational continuum—the best and brightest at one end, and the slowest and most exasperating at the other—are the ones who grab the lion's share of our attention. These are students with either abnormal promise or abnormal problems. They are not average kids, yet average describes the bulk of our student bodies. Perhaps we overlook them because *average*, by definition, fails to draw attention to itself. In fact, average *anything* tends to be rather ho-hum.

Kids on the fringe are no more or no less important than any others; but the fringe represents only a small fraction of our student bodies. Most students do not make the soccer team, do not make cheerleading, are not the valedictorian, receive no scholarships, never make the honor roll, never score a touchdown, are not selected for the homecoming court, are not abused at home, do not have a learning disability and don't have exotic hobbies. They're just average and, therefore, are often overlooked.

The average student is the type of kid who has to visit the disciplinary dean once or twice over his high school career, but the offense is usually nothing to brag about. He failed to turn in an important class assignment, even after his parents were notified; on another occasion he was caught chewing gum in chapel. He has never been involved in anything "cool," like a locker-room brawl. Physically, he is not tall, dark and handsome. He tried weightlifting, mainly to impress the girls, but gave up after two months. He has some embarrassing acne and may have to get braces next week. His picture appeared in the school newspaper, but it was a group shot. Rather nondescript, more than one teacher has marked him absent when he wasn't. He tried out for the school play and landed a minor role. A high school junior, he rides the school bus because he has no car of his own. Both of his parents work, and they have phoned the principal only once to complain about something. He knows Christ as Savior and has led one other to Christ—a child, while working with VBS one summer.

So what's my point? The point is not to get so carried away with atypical students that you overlook the vast "wasteland" sitting before you called "average." We tend to be enamored with those who have special needs, who win speech contests, who gain over five yards per carry.

Hey, I'm an individual!

Another roadblock to bonding is the tendency to always view the class as a whole, as opposed to noticing individuals who make up the whole. Do our students have to wave at us, beckoning with, "Hey, teacher, notice me"?

Do we take the time to notice a student's new glasses, braces or hairstyle? Do we follow up on their prayer requests? Do we make ourselves available to tutor after school? Have we ever visited one of our students in the hospital? Teachers who deal with their classes as groups of *individuals* find that students bond with them quickly.

Teacher, I've got a problem

Teachers who truly love their students will, as the Scriptures put it, "watch for their souls." This often involves individual counseling.

Satan will hurl plenty of fiery darts to thwart our efforts, probably because such a ministry can be so effective. "You don't have time for that," he'll whisper in our ears. "You've got papers to grade." Sometimes we have trouble finding a vacant room or office in which to counsel students; on other occasions, neither of you is free at the same time. Yet, daunting as the task may appear, it can be done. Sometimes our willingness to be used in this way boils down to our willingness to be inconvenienced.

There is an urgent need for counseling in our Christian schools. Growing up in today's world is often a painful proposition. Divorce has sabotaged the nuclear family, working mothers are the norm, the number of *latch-key* children grows and drugs have ravaged too many households. Some students are emotionally abused and unaware of the Savior's love for them, while others are trapped in sin by peer pressure. Teachers who are alert to hurting students will have no lack of ministry.

I'm a nobody

Brad spends much of his time in class with his head down. He hopes that neither his teacher nor his classmates will notice him. For the most part, they don't. He is rarely called upon, and he never volunteers. Usually Brad waits until everyone has left the classroom before asking his teacher a question, to spare himself peer ridicule. If anyone compliments him, he has difficulty accepting it. At PE, Brad will likely be found off by himself. When he returns to school after being absent, no one tells him that they missed him, because they didn't. Shunned by his classmates, Brad may cling to his teacher, knowing that at least *she* will accept him. Rejects are easy to pick out of a crowd.

Christian schools have their share of Brads. These are kids who are unnoticed, unimpressive, uninvolved and even unloved. We know, of course, that a God who notices the sparrow fall surely notices them, but the issue here is what these kids think of *themselves*. We can play a role in rebuilding their image.

Every student carries around, in the wallet of his mind, a photograph of the person he thinks he is. Some picture themselves as "most outstanding" candidates, while others see themselves as school nerds or walking acne commercials. Some are pleased with their photograph, taking it out often to admire, while others regard their photograph as so disquieting that they keep it tucked safely out of sight.

A student's self-image has enormous implications, determining whether she will blossom into a beautiful flower or fade into insignificance as a wallflower. Poor self-esteem results in eating disorders, physical diseases, aborted relationships, unfulfilled dreams and sometimes suicide. Its effects are far-reaching. Christian schools seek to cultivate students who will make an impact for Christ in a devil-dominated world, but there is little hope that students who regard themselves as worthless will ever achieve that goal.

A teacher who is open to ministering to those with low self-esteem may find the following advice helpful:

- **Help students see things from God's perspective.** Students who are believers in Christ, yet have a poor self image, need to know that they are "accepted in the Beloved" (Ephesians 1:6). While there is a self-esteem movement afoot today that tends to nudge us toward thinking of ourselves more highly than we ought (Romans 12:3), it cannot be denied that those who have committed their lives to Christ are of infinite worth to

Him. Regardless of what a young person's mirror tells him each morning, he is special.

- **Help students focus on their strengths.** A student may do commendable work in five subjects and average in one, yet dwell on the latter. A student may create award winning sculptures yet be devastated for failing to make the cheering squad. Teachers should not encourage students to deny their inadequacies but, instead, to spotlight their strengths.
- **Help students accept the unalterables.** Some things in life will never improve, and the sooner a student resigns himself to them the less his self-esteem will be wounded. If we learn not to let our prominent nose bother us, for example, others won't be bothered by it either.
- **Help students compensate.** If a student has a weakness that invites peer ridicule, he needs to be able to compensate in some way. The teacher can encourage him to take up a hobby, a sport, a musical instrument or some thing else in which he may find success. This may offset his weakness.
- **Involve students in the lives of others.** An amazing remedy for low self-esteem is a good dose of servanthood. Strangely, when kids get their eyes off themselves their problems seems to fade.

Discipline: The determining factor

Likely more than any other aspect of teaching, the way a teacher handles discipline in her class will dictate the degree to which she is able to bond with her students. It provides the touchstone—the standard by which something is tested.

When a student challenges a teacher's authority in class, all eyes are on the teacher, intent on studying her response. Will she lash back, or will she deftly defuse a potentially explosive situation? All hold their breath. Will she resort to sarcasm, or can she handle the student with a few firm yet calmly spoken words? Sometimes a mere glance or gesture will do. Will the teacher manifest the fruit of the Spirit—that morning's Bible lesson, incidentally—or will her reaction be fleshly? In the student's eyes, such occasions are everyday, gut-level Christianity in action that carry more clout than a month's worth of theory.

Some teachers are able to win their classes to such a degree that their students are reluctant to do anything that would disappoint them. Such teachers have definitely bonded with their kids. Others may not have reached such a delightful state but are working on it.

Students are constantly sizing up their teacher's sense of fair play. Are they, for example, ever allowed to appeal a punishment handed down to them? Does the teacher ever take into account extenuating circumstances? Does the teacher show any hint of empathy, able to at least imagine *why* a student might do the absurd thing he just did? The word *fair* is common currency in the conversation of most students, and they value it highly.

If a teacher is to bond with students, he must model the discipline that he seeks to impose. Christlikeness rings hollow when students are disciplined for being tardy to class and the teacher himself is often guilty of the same offense. Or when he insists upon neatness from his students, but his own desk is anything but. Or when he preaches the virtues of good preparation yet commonly resorts to showing videos because he is unready with his lesson plan.

I'm so stressed!

Another determiner of bonding is how a teacher holds up under stress. When the heat is on, some of us boil over. How do we react to an intercom interruption when we are racing to finish the lesson before the bell? Do we share with our students our disagreement with a recent school-board policy? Do we treat our last-period class as graciously as first period—before the strains of the day have set in? Do we evidence a sour attitude when we face personal financial difficulties? Some teachers ride an emotional roller coaster, while others can be relied upon even when hard times engulf them. Students are eager to learn from how we react to life's tensions, and they are attracted to those who handle them victoriously. As someone has succinctly put it: "Students close their eyes to advice but open their eyes to examples."

Believe me, I understand how you feel

Students feel a kinship with teachers who can appreciate how they feel. An empathetic teacher does not have to overlook students' failures; we are not recommending that, and neither are the students. But students do applaud a teacher who can at least understand their trials and frustrations.

- "I realize that tonight is homecoming, and I'm as excited as you are. But let's see if we can finish these problems before the bell rings."
- "It's only five minutes until lunch, and I'm starved too, but let's see if we can get to problem # 17."

- "Sounds like a thunderstorm's coming. Can you see the dark clouds in the distance? I'm glad our walkways are covered this year, so we don't get soaked anymore!"
- "I can understand why we are having a difficult time with this new method of solving equations. It took me a long time, too, when I first encountered it. But I think you'll like it once you get the hang of it."

The teacher who tries to ignore what is so obviously on the students' minds will find himself in a tug of war until he at least acknowledges their concern. Students want us to know how they feel.

Going the extra mile

Students bond readily with teachers who go the extra mile. Our Lord encourages us to this end: "Whosoever shall compel thee to go one mile, go with him two" (Matthew 5:41). This means going beyond the call of duty, and students know that a teacher genuinely loves them when he takes an interest in them at times other than when it is expected. That may include after-class help with the lesson, taking a moment between classes to pray with a student, attending a student's piano recital, attending a funeral or arranging a ride home. Students expect a teacher to give it his all when in the classroom, on his turf, but are delightedly taken aback when he shows an interest in them outside the classroom, on their turf. Such a teacher distinguishes himself in the eyes of his class. Students take an interest in the teacher who takes an interest in them.

CHAPTER FOUR

REACHING FAMILIES THROUGH THE CHRISTIAN SCHOOL

"Christian education is about more than educating minds. It is about reaching souls and touching eternity."
—Dan L. Burrell, Ed.D.

Not long ago, we asked one of our school mothers to give her testimony in chapel. She stood before the 130 or so students in our secondary school and started her talk with, "Hi, my name is Dorlynne. I am a recovering alcoholic and drug addict." The gasps in the audience among the usually hard-to-impress teens were audible. This woman embodied the stereotype of the business professional. A former paralegal, she had quit her job to serve as an administrative assistant in our school. None of the students would have ever guessed that she had a "past." She continued with her testimony to tell how she brought her young son to our ministry looking for a Christian education and some early childhood instruction. Not only did she find that for which she was looking, she met *Someone* she needed. Our faithful preschool director, an ardent soul-winner, took her into her office and shared God's plan for salvation with her and she accepted Him as Savior. From that day forward, her life dramatically changed. Today, she works for the ministry, she and her husband are active in the church, and she has broken Satan's grip on her lifestyle and interests; all because of the Christian school and a teacher who cared.

Christian education is about more than educating minds. It is about reaching souls and touching eternity. When the school is filled with clinical educators who seek only to produce superior students with decent character, we have lost sight of the spiritual mission that should fill our hearts as we interact with others. How can I use my opportunities to reach others for Christ?

Depending on the type of philosophy that your school holds, the opportunity for reaching families for Christ through the Christian school will vary. There are three primary types of enrollment philosophies that impact what kind of families will be found in your student body and will affect the potential for reaching families for Christ. The first philosophy is the *closed enrollment* philosophy. Schools having this standard generally accept only students who are members of their church.

The second type of enrollment philosophy is the *limited enrollment*. In this school, one or both of the parents must sign a statement that indicates that they have established a personal relationship with Jesus Christ and are clearly born-again believers. In limited-enrollment schools, it is not unusual to require that one or both of the parents also be active in a local church.

The third primary type of philosophy, and perhaps the most frequently used philosophy in the Christian school movement, is the *open enrollment* policy. This policy accepts students who have any or no religious background. Many times this is an intentional policy consistent with the school leadership's desire to utilize the school as an evangelistic tool. Generally, the only requirement for entrance beyond the regular academic screens is that the parents must agree to abide by and support the school's spiritual mission.

There are also three primary types of Christian schools that can be categorized by sponsorship. There is the *denominational* school that is often overseen by and designed specifically for the students from an association of churches that have the same denominational affiliation. There is the *church-sponsored* school, which is sponsored by, governed primarily by and often located in the facilities of a local church. The third type of school is the *board-sponsored* school that is usually founded by a group of concerned parents and business people as an alternative to government schools and who desire a school with spiritual values and philosophy. All three of these types of schools can make a significant effort in reaching the families of their student body for Christ.

No matter what type of school you have, you can reach others for Christ. In the limited-enrollment church-school, you will find parents who have "played the game" but do not truly know Christ. You will also find homes that are at various levels of spiritual maturity or function. For those who have open-enrollment schools, the issue of evangelism through the school is not only an opportunity, but an obligation. How can we *not* invite those we serve to accept Christ?

This chapter will give you ten specific ways in which you can reach families for Christ. Not all of them will apply to every type or philosophy of school; others will apply to any school. There are plenty of Dorlynnes in our school family, and who better to reach them than the Christian educator.

1. **Gather as much spiritual history about your students and their families as possible early in the school year.**

On the student application, you may want to ask the question: "If you died today, do you believe you would go to heaven?" And follow up with a second question that says: "If you answered *yes*, please explain the basis for your answer." You may want to make it a multiple choice by asking them to respond to the first question with several options, such as: "(1) Yes, (2) No, (3) I hope so, (4) I'd prefer not to answer." With that response you should have a pretty good idea as to the salvation of the individual. Few people who are truly born-again will ever be offended about answering a question in regard to their salvation. We *want* to tell others, and if we don't, there's something wrong! You could also ask if they attend church, what church they attend, or for a paragraph describing their religious beliefs or heritage.

Another tack is to ask the student to relate their spiritual heritage on a student application or on an early assignment at the beginning of the year. Notations in the spiritual records file of the student can be kept. It is advisable to have a spiritual record dossier kept in the cumulative folder to help administrators and other teachers. If the parents are members of a cult or if they have been presented with the gospel, it is good for future teachers or administrators involved in family counseling to have access to that information.

Additional information may be gained through the enrollment interview, interaction with the student, and even student responses during chapel or Bible class invitations. The alert teacher will be able to quickly assess the spiritual condition of a student and, more than likely, the condition of his home. This is not judging but rather the gathering of important information for future ministry.

An additional note: In the secondary school, it is easy to assume that some other teacher is taking care of gathering the spiritual history of the students. Assignments should be specific, such as having the homeroom teacher or the Bible teacher be responsible for each grade or class. Some larger schools are able to add the position of campus chaplain to assist with gathering information. But it should be noted that *every* teacher should have the spiritual condition of his or her students on their heart every day.

2. Require each teacher to visit in the home of all his or her homeroom students.

This may seem a bit arbitrary, but most Christian educators understand that ministry in a Christian school is different from that in a government school. There are responsibilities for ministry that go above and beyond the call of duty. There are several good reasons for requiring home visits.

First, it allows the teacher to see firsthand the environment in which the students learn and live. One of our teachers once visited the home of a new student who was showing some rather bizarre behavior. When she visited the home of the pre-adolescent child, she noticed that the parents seemed rather nonplused about her visit and oblivious to their son's progress or lack thereof. The teacher asked the boy if she might see his room. The boy very excitedly assented and gleefully directed her down the hall. When he opened the door, to her amazement, she saw that the room was painted black and was illuminated by black lights. On the walls were various symbols of hard rock bands and occult symbols. Directly above the boy's bed was a pin-up poster of a scantily clad model that would best be described as pornographic. While she tried not to appear shocked in front of the student, she quickly exited and returned to the room where the parents were and arranged to speak to them privately.

When she expressed her concern to the parents, they seemed rather unconcerned, stating that they felt that a child's room was the place for his self-expression and that they rarely entered it and did not care what he did in it. It became quickly apparent that they had lied on several questions that would have revealed a non-supportive attitude on the parental application. To make a long story short, the boy was withdrawn from the school in a few days due to the conflict that swiftly emerged from the divergent philosophies between the school and home.

A home visit also gives the opportunity to determine key spiritual facts about the family. It will be quickly obvious to the discerning teacher whether or not spiritual priorities are practiced within the home. In addition, observing child-parent interaction, sibling interaction or if any unusual living conditions are present (i.e., grandparents living at home, adult siblings living at home, unusual work situations, etc.)— which may provide the teacher with helpful insight into the home environment.

The home visit demonstrates a significant commitment to communication and information gathering to the parents. Most parents are surprised to be approached by a teacher for a home visit. Not all parents will desire that the teacher visit in their home, which is their right, but that also can communicate something to the teacher. The level of commitment that would inspire the teacher to use personal time for building relationships between home and school impresses most parents.

It should be noted at this juncture that there should be several "rules" surrounding the practice of visiting in homes. Let me list a few here:

- The visit should be pre-arranged. Few people in our present culture appreciate drop-in visits. Most parents would like a time to prepare.
- The visit should be relatively brief. Thirty minutes to one hour should be ample time.
- The visit should be positive. Make the experience encouraging. Bring good news of improved conduct or effort or even an example of good work.
- Ask the student to show you his or her room. Most kids like to show off their stuff, and this gives the teacher an opportunity to give the student some personal attention during the visit.
- Never indulge in a critique of the school, the administration or other teachers—past or present. Should the conversation take a turn in that direction, the teacher should quickly and authoritatively change the subject. If they persist, a gentle, "It wouldn't be appropriate for me to discuss this topic as a professional," will generally end the effort.
- Ask the parents about their spiritual heritage, church affiliation and commitment to Christ. If it becomes apparent that they do not know Christ as Savior, then ask if you could share your personal testimony with them. This will usually lead into an opportunity to present the plan of salvation.
- If possible, conclude the visit with prayer. This provides a spiritual conclusion to the appointment and also "announces" that the home visit is over.

- The home visit is one of the most effective ways in which teachers can make a spiritual impact on the families in the Christian school. Every visit should conclude with an invitation to your church if the family does not have a church home or the suggestion that they should call on your church if they are ever in need of spiritual assistance.

3. Put all school parents on the church mailing list.
Most churches send out monthly newsletters and usually special announcements for extraordinary events. It is essential that you constantly remind your parents that there are church functions that they might want to attend. If you are in a school that is not sponsored by a single church, you may want to invite local churches that share your doctrinal positions to submit announcements for inclusion in the school newspaper or monthly update.

4. Develop music and drama groups that can be used in ministry.
Many churches enjoy having youth choirs, ensembles and even small groups and soloists to present special numbers during their worship services. There are few things more impressive than well-rehearsed and well-groomed young people singing about the Lord. This is an effective way to train your young people to be active in local church ministry. It will build their confidence and skills, provide terrific public relations for your school and will encourage parents to visit church services where their young people are scheduled to minister.

Many churches are now utilizing short drama vignettes as part of an introduction to a sermon or to teach a spiritual principle. These take the form of skits, readers' theater or monologues. Developing a repertoire of several options and presenting these to local pastors or the pastor of your sponsoring church, may encourage them to invite a student or group of students to minister through this effective tool during a worship service. Again, you can anticipate the parents coming to the service to see their children minister.

5. Assign a Christian-School Day for your church.
This can be one of the most effective ways through which you can reach school families. Christian Schools of Palm Beach County, Florida, has scheduled a Christian Education Week in their county for over a decade. The local government has even officially recognized this week. A joint ad by the nearly 20 schools in their organization is placed in the local newspaper. In addition, they print very impressive 4-color bulletin inserts and supply them free of charge to any local churches that would like to participate. In many churches, special recognition of Christian schoolteachers, students and families is scheduled.

Our ministry, which is a Christian school sponsored by our Independent Baptist church, has a tradition of establishing an annual Berean Christian School Day. (In recent years, due to the size of our church and our school, we have had to assign 2 services per Sunday for 2 Sundays in order to accommodate the crowds.) In planning this day, it is our objective to give every student in our Christian school who does not have a regular church home an assignment for that day in church. Some serve as greeters, others serve as ushers, the special music is provided by the students, and we conclude with a school-wide choir and recitation of a chapter of Scripture. This involves significant planning and some rehearsal, but these are traditionally the best-attended services of our year with the exceptions of Christmas and Easter services. On these Sundays, I preach a sermon that relates to the family but which also includes a salvation emphasis. It is safe to say that over the years we have seen literally scores of families make a commitment to Christ and/or to being a part of our church as a result of an annual recognition service.

We make an effort to encourage students who are active in good Bible-preaching ministries to attend their church services and not come to our services that day. It is unethical for Bible-preaching churches to compete with each other for faithful believers who have a commitment to their church. There shouldn't be a penalty for students who are not able to participate on this Sunday.

A nice follow-up letter is an appropriate gesture in which the pastor thanks the school parents for visiting in the services and encourages them to come again in the future. In addition, you may want to have a response card available in the pews on which the visiting parents can check a response like: "I'm interested in more information about your church," or: "I'm interested in knowing how I can go to heaven when I die." These provide the opportunity for a follow-up visit into the home by a member of your evangelism ministry.

You will find that the more times you can get school parents into the church, the more likely they will be to start feeling at home in your church. You must not be satisfied with that, however, the church must have a strategy for evangelization and discipleship that will cause a long-term spiritual impact. Remember that you are not trying to draw a crowd, you are trying to build a church family.

6. Plan a Sunday or Wednesday series that would interest parents.

When the pastor knows he is going to preach a sermon that will be a help to school families, a general announcement should be sent home. It could even be featured on a school marquis. A sermon or series on child rearing, discipline, character, marriage or communication in the home will attract many school parents to be a part of the service.

7. Discourage church-school conflicts.

There will be times when the schedules of churches and Christian schools will come into conflict. This can be controlled to some extent if a church-sponsored school will adopt a master calendar policy. When I was a boy growing up in Missouri and still in public schools, many of the teachers had a policy that they would not give homework on Wednesday nights, because it was traditionally a church night set aside for prayer meetings and Bible study. For many years this was the norm in Christian schools, but in recent years it has become an exception. Homework is important, but the thoughtful Christian school administration should find a way to reduce homework loads on Wednesday nights, or perhaps at least give some grace to those who actually attend and give evidence (a church bulletin with the date on it or the signature of a church official) that they were in church. This is certainly reasonable and eliminates an excuse that some parents might have for not attending a midweek service.

Additional consideration can be shown when there is a revival service or missions conference scheduled at the sponsoring church or in a church where a significant number of your students attend. Balance is always important to a successful educational experience, and by allowing some latitude on the issue of homework on church nights, you will be encouraging church attendance, eliminating stress for families and making an important statement regarding the priority of church participation.

If your school uses church facilities, you will need to take extra caution that you do not allow a church-vs.-Christian-school mentality to take place. I have seen schoolteachers write large, rather unkind, signs on chalkboards telling Sunday school teachers not to use the chalkboards. I have seen Sunday school teachers allow young kids to sit at the teacher's desk and rummage through the drawers or leave the classroom in a shambles for Monday morning. There needs to be great consideration between those who use the facility during the week and those who use it on the weekends. The subtle message that there is conflict between the church and school can create a hostile climate that will impede ministry and participation on the part of school parents. When school parents become resentful of the church, then there is a problem. The administration of the school needs to locate the problem and address it authoritatively.

8. Some teachers may be able to make specific interventions in the home that will at least allow the student to come to church.

Not every parent will come to the church. No strategy or formula can ensure 100 percent participation. But that does not mean that the student cannot come to church. For years, our family has usually had at least one extra child in our car as we head to church each Sunday. It is often the thoughtful intervention of a neighbor, family member or schoolteacher that rescues a child from growing up without attendance at a good Bible-preaching church. I recently had lunch with a man who is now well into his 70s. He has been a member of his Baptist church for six decades and a deacon for over 40 years. I asked him if he was reared in a Christian home and he told me that he hadn't been. His exposure to church first came through a lady who was teaching Sunday school at his church, drove by his house on a Sunday morning and saw him playing in his yard. Later that afternoon, she came by and asked him to visit church with her the next Sunday. He did and brought his brother. Every Sunday for a year, she picked the brothers up and during that year, they found the Lord. Now, over half a century later, they are still serving the Lord all because one teacher noticed.

Most of us will have students in our class who do not go to church on Sunday and their parents have little interest in taking them. Yes, it will require a little effort and will be inconvenient at times, but if we could make the difference in just one life, would it not be worth it?

9. Speak of your personal involvement in church in front of parents and students.

I believe that Christian schoolteachers should also be active in ministry at their local church. One of my pet peeves is to hear a teacher say that because they minister at a Christian school through the week, they don't have a ministry in the local church on Sundays. Yes, full-time vocational ministry is taxing and is indeed ministry. Yet many of the Sunday school teachers, choir members and AWANA workers in the local church are also hard-working citizens who put in the same hours as we do and still find time for ministry in the local church. The Christian schoolteacher who has a ministry in the local church will find that he can find opportunities to invite school parents and family members to join in their ministry. Whether it is a Sunday school fellowship, a pro-life walkathon, a ladies retreat, or a father and son campout, there will be times when the teacher can reach out to the school families and invite them to come along.

10. Set a goal and pray over it.

If every Christian schoolteacher would make it a goal to reach just one family over the course of an entire school year for Christ, can you imagine the collective impact that such an effort could have? While my wife and I are no longer classroom teachers, we recently asked the Lord to lead us to a family in our community whom we could reach for Christ and see become a part of our church. My son plays on the local little league team, and we sensed that the Lord could lay someone on our heart through that organization. Within a couple of weeks, we noticed a sharp family with beautiful children. Our son and their son were about the same size and shared a similar skill level. Before long, they became friends. We introduced ourselves to the family and found that we shared similar values and interests. It was my joy several months later to baptize the mother and father and to celebrate a new friendship and their fresh relationship with Jesus Christ. The Lord had answered our prayers, and we were richer for it!

Yes, we must maintain a professional relationship with our school students and parents. But that professional distance does not have to come at the expense of their soul. We *can* reach parents for Christ and that should be our goal and our calling.

Chapter Five

Student Motivation

"The first ingredient in producing motivated students is making sure that you are motivated. Excitement is contagious, but you've got to have it before you can infect someone else with it."

—Philip C. Johnson, Ph.D.

You enter the classroom and are faced with numerous empty desks. You know that it will only be a matter of minutes before they are filled with students—your charges, the souls that you are assigned to motivate and inspire. What a seemingly impossible task. The task seems even more daunting when you realize that *you* were barely motivated to get out of bed yourself this morning. So how are you going to stimulate *them*? Cattle prods, while effective, are generally frowned upon for classroom use. (They really are more of an outdoor tool.) So you've got to come up with some way to get these students excited, passionate, or at least get them to show up for your class.

From kindergarten through high school, student motivation is tricky stuff. There are developmental stages, certain personalities and specific subjects that require very little work on our part to produce high levels of motivation. There are, however, many more times than we'd like, instances when we're not sure we can see even the tiniest flicker of life in our students. While every age provides unique challenges, this chapter will deal with some general principles of how to generate students who care about their school-work, their walk with Christ and others.

Start with Yourself

Well? What about it? Are you motivated? Are you inspiring? Be honest, no one's looking, and I promise not to tell. When your class sees you first thing in the morning, do they get the impression that you are excited to be with them, or do they detect that, given the opportunity, you'd just as soon be at the dentist? Of course we all know that there are times when a root canal might seem to be the better option, but that's a whole different chapter isn't it? The first ingredient in producing motivated students is making sure that *you* are motivated. If I'm not terribly excited about boiled cabbage (and believe me, I'm not), it would be very difficult to try to cause someone else to be excited about it. Excitement is contagious, but you've got to have it before you can infect someone else with it. Here are some things to consider when it comes to your responsibility in setting the initial attitude for your motivated classroom.

Your personal motivation is an outgrowth of the belief that what you are doing has significance and lasting value

As Christian educators, we need to remind ourselves on a daily basis that what we're doing has eternal value; it is an endeavor that is truly worthy of investing your life. I can think of precious few occupations that provide the depth of opportunity for impacting lives as Christian education offers. If you ever, for just a moment, begin to doubt this, let me remind you of a few life-changing opportunities

Christian educators have: the chance to change students' lives in the areas of salvation, Christian growth and future Christian service. You cannot help but become excited when you take the time to contemplate the impression you can have on individuals and eternity. Each time a student enters your life, take a few minutes to look down the road a bit. Ask God to give you a heart and vision for this child and for his or her future. You never know how and in what capacity God will use the little urchin who spends most of his time sitting outside the principal's office. He could become the next major evangelist or political figure. And to be honest, it's sort of nice to have friends in high places!

Personal motivation takes preparation

Nothing saps the life out of teaching like not knowing what in the world you're doing. When a teacher is not prepared, it opens up opportunities for your class to implement their own plans. And believe you me, they always have a plan—most of which are just plain scary. Further, being prepared sends the message to your students that you care about what you're doing. It tells them that they are valuable to you and that what they will be learning that day is important.

Think back to the last time that you really prepared a lesson. You probably had visual enhancements, interactive student activities and charming illustrations. If you're like most people, you probably couldn't wait to present that lesson. You probably felt confident and exhilarated. As a result of your preparation, your anticipation and excitement were easily transferred to your students. So, it comes down to a choice as to how you're going to prepare. I won't lie to you, it takes time; but the results are well worth the time invested.

Personal motivation takes prayer

No one always feels on top of the world every day of their life. (With the exception of my third-grade teacher, Mrs. Hinkle, but that may very well have been the result of her asthma medication combined with her fondness for Twinkies.) In the real world, the Christian educator must submit himself, his emotions and his personal desires to God daily. Again, this is a matter of choice and commitment. Central to a person's success in maintaining their motivation level and emotional stability is their personal walk with Christ. We would think someone foolish if they complained about their incapacitated car that was simply out of gas. Similarly, Christians, especially Christian teachers, cannot expect to run well when their spiritual lives are on empty. Time must be spent in daily Bible study and prayer. In addition to this, I see no harm in the occasional Twinkie.

Motivation takes personal involvement

It is difficult to become excited about students if you don't care about them. Get to know your students. Crawl inside their heads and discover what's important to them. Conduct interest surveys to identify what excites them and where their values lie. Go to one of their baseball games or ballet recitals. Show them that you care. There is a proper balance in being able to love and understand your students without becoming their "buddy" or "friend." Remember that the key is to be involved with *them*. They don't have to know all that much about *you* except for the fact that you love them. Keep a good portion of the rest of your life a bit of a mystery to them. This mystery will also enable your students to tell much more interesting stories about you later in life. And I know that any future embellishment my former students come up with about me is bound to be more interesting than my real life.

Academic Motivation

Once you have gained a grip on your own ability to create some classroom motivation, you must turn your attention to the students. Obviously, one of the major areas worthy of student motivation is academics. Twelve years or more of basic education can become laborious. We have all witnessed students who have had good years and bad years. Parents continually complain at various stages that their child has simply lost his or her motivation. So, how can teachers help keep students motivated academically throughout their educational careers? Student attitudes depend on so many factors that there is certainly no pat answer to this. Face it, people: In this case, students are complex. Much of the difficulty we experience regarding student attitudes is directly related to spiritual concerns, which we will discuss later. There are, however, some overriding principles that can be used to keep students headed in the right direction.

Help students see the big picture

Students who view their academic careers as just one meaningless day after another will soon lose steam. Students and people in general need to see how all the pieces fit together. Can you imagine trying to put together a 10,000-piece puzzle without the benefit of the picture on the front of the box? Personally, I'd probably put together about four pieces before I decided to go out for pizza and forget the whole thing. The principle applies to students who often can't see how one grade, one class or even one chapter relates to another or to the rest of life. Make learning relevant for students. Take that ever-so-tired-and-worn-out first grader, and let him know that the numbers that he is adding today will be subtracted next year and multiplied the next. And if he really gets good at numbers, there's a little thing called the stock market that he may find to be very interesting in the future. Can we say, "Early retirement," or, "Condo in Bermuda"? Of course I'm being ridiculous, but the point is valid. Motivation often comes from understanding where one is going. Excitement increases as the picture comes more and more into focus. Provide this for students.

As our students become more mature in Christ, great motivation can be derived from an understanding of how the things students are learning can be applied to honoring Christ. It should be a major goal of every teacher to get students to this point.

Provide variety

If someone forced you to sit in a desk and made you listen to yourself for an hour, how scary would that be? And yet scores of students endure this day after day. I have come to realize that it is much more fun to be the one talking than the one doing the listening. (Which basically means that most of us have found ourselves to be the most interesting people we know!) Many who have continued their education after starting their educational careers have found that once they are back in a classroom situation, they suffer from occasional boredom. Use that reminder to be certain that you don't inflict this on your own students. Use some variety in your teaching style. Make good use of visuals and incorporate review games when appropriate. Turn routine assignments into fascinating projects. Use videos that can visually transport students to the nether regions of the world. Ask specialists to come in as guest speakers. There are literally hundreds of ways to spice up a classroom and light a fire under students, and there are many books available that will provide you with ideas. Unfortunately, because we all get so busy, it is easy to fall into an easily prepared, predictable, dull pattern. Just a little time spent in planning can dramatically change the direction of your class.

Help students get organized

Not much is more demoralizing than always being behind, unprepared or looking for homework assignments. On the first day of school, spend considerable time teaching and training students in the lost art of organization. You will be amazed how the motivation level will rise when students are organized. It's much more pleasant to have assignments completed and to actually know where those assignments are than to spend time searching vainly through the dark and mysterious corners of one's desk—where one is more likely to find the remains of last week's Spam sandwich than today's algebra assignment.

Insist that students use assignment pads. Encourage color-coded folders for different classes. Remind students that it's OK to throw things away once in a while. There is no reason that a classroom desk needs to become a time capsule, and the fair market value on last month's spelling test is not likely to increase.

Help students understand their own significance

Nothing will destroy motivation more effectively than when a student struggles with his or her own significance.

Though this can be a factor at any age, personal significance is usually more of an issue with junior-high students.
Junior-high students enter a world that is very different than
that of elementary school. They leave an environment in
which they usually had the same teacher all day long and
were capable of making some kind of impression on that
teacher. Now they are participating in a world of multiple
teachers and they don't have near the opportunity to make
an impression. It is very easy for students in this situation
to begin to believe that they don't matter—that they are
insignificant. In this climate, it doesn't take long for students to become apathetic. To them it seems easier to give
up than to feel successful. The junior and senior high
schoolteacher needs to pay particular attention to this reality. There are simply fewer opportunities for junior-high
students to *shine* and make an impact. All students need to
feel a proper sense of their own worth. The teacher needs
to look for opportunities to allow students to excel and
find their own unique niche. Ambition comes from an understanding of past victories and a sense of being conse-
quential in one's new circumstances.

Now, having said all of this, let me point out that foundational to all of this and key to any sense of self-worth is
the possession of a right relationship with Jesus Christ.
Without an understanding that all significance comes from
one's position in Christ, all else that a student may accomplish will really be meaningless.

Spiritual Motivation

Unique and crucial to our educational ministries is the
spiritual motivation of students. In fact, one could make
the argument that spiritual motivation is essential to all

other motivations. Of course spiritual motivation depends initially on a student's relationship with Christ. Teachers should never take for granted that their students have all trusted Christ as their Savior, no matter how long that child has been in a Christian school.

Never assume

I remember distinctly working with a wonderful 14-year-old boy for several years (though, admittedly, he was not always wonderful and he was not always 14). He was the son of a pastor and, for all intents and purposes, a model student. I never gave this particular student's spiritual life a second thought. One day this boy asked to talk to me in private. He burst into tears and confessed that he had never trusted Christ as his Savior and had been living a life that was nothing more than a lie. He told me that his parents were not aware of half of what he was doing behind their backs. Fortunately, the Holy Spirit had brought him to a point of repentance, but certainly not because of my prodding. I had never even asked this boy about his relationship with Jesus. I had just assumed. I had judged him to be a Christian based on circumstantial evidence.

As Christian educators, we need to be proactive in asking those important questions about the eternity of our students, regardless of their outward behavior or the integrity of their family tree.

Be a model

Aside from a student's personal relationship with Jesus, one of the most potentially powerful influences on student spiritual motivation is the model presented by adults in the student's life. Aside from parents, no adult is more prevalent in a student's life than his teacher. Take advantage of this opportunity. Be a model of a spiritually-motivated person. Students need to see what Christ is doing in you without you being too self-revealing. Students don't need to know what shade of Miss Clairol you use or how many warts you have on your toes; they need to know what Christ is doing in your life on a daily basis. As they witness the effect Christ has on your yielded life, it will no doubt impact them. This is especially true if you have cultivated a proper and caring relationship with your students that has created the all-important mentality of: "I want to be just like you." Being a model does not mean that you have to be perfect. Much can be learned by the student who sees us as honest, fallible people who have a desire to grow and to be like Christ. Never underestimate the powerful tool of *positive influence.*

Make Christian service practical

Many students may have a desire to please God but may have no idea of how to go about pleasing Him. Somehow we have succeeded in teaching our young people that pleasing God is a big mystery. Pleasing God is certainly not an adventure similar to finding a needle in the haystack. Opportunities to please God abound. We've communicated to our students that pleasing God involves prayer and Bible reading and this is true, but it's not all. Students need something concrete to help them get fired up for God. "Even so faith, if it hath not works, is dead, being alone" (James 2:17). Teach your students that good works are evidence of their faith. Encourage your students to cut a neighbor's grass, visit a nursing home, teach a Sunday school class or make dinner for a shut-in. Have students use any talents they may possess in a church service. Show them the opportunities! Get their eyes off themselves and onto others. There's really no better way to build excitement in spiritual things and to develop a caring heart for others than through service.

Personal Bible Study

Motivating students to study the Word of God is probably one of our most important and most difficult tasks. In our Christian schools, we routinely have Bible time and memorize Scripture. Unfortunately we often stop there. Many of our kids are consistently spoon fed God's Word and develop neither the skills to study God's Word on their own nor the hunger for it. Try presenting your class with passages of Scripture for study that are directly applicable to their age. Help students discover biblical truths for themselves. Don't always give them answers, but guide them through the process of discovery. When students do uncover truths, rejoice with them. And finally, share with your students the truths that you have found through your own personal Bible study. Once again, this is your opportunity to be a model for your class.

There are many other areas of a student's life about which educators would love to see students become motivated. Included in this list are items such as sports, music, clubs and social life. We need to help our young people develop the attitude of doing all things as unto the Lord. I Corinthians 10: 31 encourages: "Whether therefore ye eat, or drink, or whatsoever ye do, do all to the glory of God." This type of development takes time, and educators must patiently guide their students toward this goal. No kindergartner will automatically understand that principle, but they will understand the principle of pleasing you. Never underestimate the power you possess in student motivation just by cultivating a *relationship* with your students. Along with a child's parents, you can be one of a child's first, earthly examples of Christ.

Students often begin their journey toward motivated success and faithfulness as a result of wanting to please a particular teacher. They work harder and jump higher in order not to disappoint that much-loved teacher. As they grow up and grow in their spiritual life, they will be able to transfer their desire to please you into a desire to please God. This is especially true as the teacher continually points them toward the One that they can please the most.

CHAPTER SIX

CLIMATE CONTROL: CREATING A CLASSROOM ATMOSPHERE THAT MINIMIZES MISBEHAVIOR

"To know what to do when students are unruly is certainly helpful, no question, but to forestall it from surfacing altogether is far more practical."

—Paul Tatham, M.S.

Becky Williams eased into her seat for the third session of the day. Turning to Sherry, also a new teacher at Morningside Christian Academy, she shared her excitement over her first teaching opportunity. Sherry had much to accomplish during this week of pre-school faculty orientation; yet, like her colleague Becky, she eagerly anticipated opening day.

Principal Joe Bradley entered the room, welcomed the teachers to his session and opened in prayer. His topic was discipline, "the bedrock of all teaching," as he put it.

Principal Bradley explained that well-ordered classes are one of the distinctives of Christian education and a primary reason why parents seek us out. He cited specific examples of the sad state of student decorum in public education, elaborated on the 1969 Tinker case and other Supreme Court rulings that served to shift the burden of proof from the student to the school, and even touched on Horace Mann's now ludicrous claim that if state-run schools were adopted in America there would be no need for prisons.

After laying the groundwork, Mr. Bradley launched into an explanation of the particular discipline system used at Morningside Christian. It was a simple, yet sensible, system, and both teachers felt they had a working grasp of its mechanics and were ready to use it on opening day.

Nine months later, as Becky and Sherry were sharing a fast-food supper together and planning their end-of-year classroom parties, they reflected back on that opening session. Although they felt they had been well briefed on their school's disciplinary expectations and the means to accomplish them, they knew something was missing. After recounting some of their failures, they wished out loud that Mr. Bradley had given them some pointers regarding discipline *prevention.* That would have spared them several embarrassing situations, perhaps, and made their first year more enjoyable.

Teacher training in classroom management seems to focus more on how to handle discipline problems than on how to avoid them in the first place. What teachers really need is help with creating a class climate in which misbehavior is held to a minimum. To know what to do when students are unruly is certainly helpful, no question, but to forestall it from surfacing altogether is far more practical.

Viewing Discipline as a Ministry

Keeping misbehavior from surfacing begins with the teacher's mindset. A teacher's attitude toward discipline, in and of itself, may largely dictate his success. Rather than viewing decorum as a *purpose* of teaching, a teacher may mistakenly regard it as a *problem* of teaching—something on par with recess duty or grading papers. Keeping order is relegated to the status of an occupational hazard.

The teacher who treats class discipline like a pesky fly guarantees himself more flies. His attitude will only inspire the students to deeper depths of depravity; for once they realize their behavior can exasperate, and thus control the teacher, some will redouble their efforts. This teacher has yet to learn that discipline must always be part of his lesson plan. Every teacher, even the best, must contend with it daily, so one might as well accept it as a given. As long as students possess the *old nature*, and even Christian kids have to contend with that, they will always be prone to test the limits of authority. The wise teacher accepts this fact and views with healthy acceptance his charge to maintain order.

The teacher with the most mature attitude of all, however, takes discipline a step further. He not only acquiesces to its inevitability, but he sees it positively—as an opportunity for ministry. Actually, he considers discipline as part of his curriculum, an outcome to be planned for as much as integrating biblical principles. Teaching students to sit still and concentrate is as much a part of the curriculum as understanding chemistry's periodic table. Indeed, the one must precede the other. Consequently, when misbehavior does surface, this teacher is not flustered. He knows that it is part of the warp and woof of his lesson.

To perceive discipline positively is to be prepared for teaching. Such a teacher relishes the awesome opportunity to shape young lives while there is hope—before the concrete of character fully hardens.

Getting to Know You

"Be prepared." More than just a Boy Scout motto, preparation is indispensable in preventing discipline problems.

Those teachers unwilling to devote the time necessary to planning strategy are usually forced to devote more time later picking up the pieces. Simply put, they learn the costly lesson that it is better to *pre*pare than to *re*pair.

Part of that preparation for discipline is knowing one's students. This entails everything from learning what makes junior-high kids so animated, to merely learning their names. Just as a jockey studies all he can about horses, so a teacher studies her students. The better a teacher knows her students, the better she will be able to train them.

A teacher must, first, know her students collectively. This encompasses a broad grasp of basic age characteristics. She will know, for instance, that junior-high students have values, interests, strengths, needs and thinking processes that differ from senior-high students. She may learn that although research confirms that fifth grade is the most deceitful age, males and females tend to be equally devious throughout their school careers. The fact that upper-elementary students memorize more easily than upper high-school students does not surprise her. Mental, physical, social and spiritual features distinguish each age group—from primaries to seniors. Too many teachers, sadly, enter their profession brimming with naive idealism, unaware of the realities facing them.

To be aware of the evolution of behavior is helpful. When a child is young, his behavior is dominated by maturational factors. As he grows older, experiential factors step to the fore. Thus, behavior becomes less predictable. The teacher of adolescents, knowing this, is less apt to be frustrated.

To a certain extent, a teacher must identify with the age group that she teaches. Hudson Taylor, the nineteenth-century missionary to China, was known for his emphasis on cultural identity. Taylor claimed that if one is to make an impact he must attain 70 percent identification. This is not to imply, of course, that a middle-aged teacher must adopt the hairstyles, dress, mannerisms and jargon of his junior-high students. Far from it. Understanding the group does not mean joining it. It simply means that a teacher must empathize with his young charges. When they talk about collecting baseball cards, he can understand, if not share, their excitement. When they moan over the unfortunate alignment of three tests scheduled on the same day following a crucial playoff game they wanted to watch the evening before, he understands their consternation. Winning students involves some cross-cultural identification, some stretching.

Group characteristics are important, but even more so are the individuals who comprise the group. A teacher does not teach a group, after all, but rather individuals who happen to be gathered into a group. The better a teacher knows each student, individually, the better she will be able to manage them and meet their needs.

To accomplish this, the teacher must learn as much as possible about each student in her class before opening day. She must study their files, talk to previous teachers, etc. Some teachers, however, take issue here, claiming that any preconceived notions about a student will hopelessly bias them and dash all hopes of equitable treatment. But that fear is often unfounded. To an educator, foreknowledge can be the determining factor in starting the year aright. It can keep her from making mistakes others have made, as well as yield clues regarding managing behavior and learning styles. The wise teacher welcomes all available information, ready to use it in positive and constructive ways. To be forewarned is to be forearmed. The value of such prior knowledge outweighs the limited danger of preconceived bias—the so-called Rosenthal Effect.

Once school starts, the teacher will want to build on that database. Some survey their students' hobbies, travel experiences, favorite foods, birthdays, parent occupations, church affiliations and the like; others take the extra effort to visit each student's home, knowing that such contact will build a bridge of communication and perhaps shed light on why some students behave the way they do.

Knowing students individually means that a teacher learns which corrective measures are effective with which students. To Stephanie, for example, denying her recess might be no punishment at all. To Randy, on the other hand, it may be the only punishment that will bridle his impulsiveness. A mere look or gesture is enough to give Bradley pause, while private counsel is what works for Lindsey. To some extent, discipline must be individually tailored.

Routines: New every morning!

Establishing basic classroom routines can go a long way toward preventing discipline problems. Before the school year begins, the farsighted teacher maps out his game plan for classroom management, and this certainly will include standard operating procedures for much of the mundane. Especially important in the elementary grades, such *modus operandi* makes for a smooth-running class. Children need to know how to line up for restroom breaks, the way to distribute and collect papers, or the proper way to shelve lunch boxes. Without such fundamental routines in place, confusion and frustration is sure to ensue.

New teachers would be well advised to inquire of veterans as to the routines they use. Those who have taught for a few years will proudly share those techniques they have honed to perfection. Their kids can unpack their belongings into their cubbyhole with the precision of a West Point drill team!

Unlike adults, children love routines. To them, routines produce a sense of order and security. Far from drudgery, children feel safe and businesslike operating within prescribed guidelines. They eagerly comply and, once into the school year, routines become second nature. Then Heaven help the substitute teacher who tries to deviate! Adults tend to forget that what to them is now a tedious routine, they once considered a thrilling new approach. In fact, to a youngster a routine is excitingly "new" every morning! I remember as a youngster the thrill of learning how to tie my shoes and grabbing every opportunity to practice. Somehow, I now no longer experience that thrill every morning when dressing!

Routines are a means to an end. Kids seem to know instinctively that the more quickly and efficiently their papers are collected, for example, the sooner they will be able to begin an enjoyable lesson. Basic routines free up the teacher so that she can do what she was hired to do—teach. They save time and take the guesswork out of classroom logistics.

Fogged in

Preventive discipline sometimes involves something rather esoteric: awareness. This is the ability to effectively teach while simultaneously monitoring audience feedback. Though a quality that is essentially part of one's very nature—either a teacher has it or he doesn't—to a certain extent awareness can be nurtured and cultivated.

Rookie teachers often lack awareness. Like an inexperienced actor on the stage, he may be so intent upon remembering his lines that he forgets the audience. He may be so consumed with his notes, overhead projector, or even his delivery that he may seemingly forget all about those for whom the lesson is intended. Some students may be doodling, perhaps seated directly under his nose; others yawn and whisper to neighbors. But the teacher drones on, oblivious to the undercurrent of restlessness.

Awareness is a teacher's sixth sense. It is the ability to be simultaneously cognizant of students in the back corner of the classroom and those in the front row. The teacher with an acute sense of awareness has developed peripheral vision and hearing. He can be lecturing toward one side of the room while keeping an eye on the other side. He can quietly deal with one individual's question while eavesdropping on two whisperers who consider themselves safely out of earshot. He can work at his desk while maintaining an invisible finger on developments far beyond his reach. He can stand at the chalkboard, back turned, yet make his presence felt throughout the classroom.

The aware teacher never becomes so engrossed in one student's question that he loses touch with the rest of the class. While answering that student's question, either privately or in a class discussion, the teacher faces the rest of the class, scanning the horizon for signs of inattention or disruption. Like an orchestra conductor, a teacher may be leading one section while eyeing the orchestra as a whole. He must be ever alert to all the student activity that surrounds him.

The aware teacher learns to control his class through deft manipulation of unseen strings. He quells a potential interruption with a stare or dramatic pause. While lecturing, he stations himself momentarily beside a troublemaker who appears ready to make his move. Forsaking the lectern, he circulates around the room and strolls freely down aisles. He silences disruptions with hand signals, a snap of the fingers, a touch or simply a disapproving glance. The aware teacher is in control.

The unaware teacher, on the other hand, encourages not only horseplay but also dishonesty. To tempt students by placing them with an unobservant teacher is to tempt them unfairly. The major finding of the classic Hartshorne and May study on children's honesty (1928) was that even children who belong to character-developing organizations, such as Boy Scouts and church groups, will cheat if the pressure is strong enough and the risk is low. In fact, it was found that intrinsic morality is of little deterrent value to youngsters. Even teachers in Christian schools must be alert to the frailties of the flesh.

Just coasting along

A teacher seeking to minimize misbehavior never coasts. Never. The teacher unwilling to spend the time necessary to keep his class gainfully employed at all times will find himself in deep trouble.

Some teachers coast on a regular basis. If the students have survived a particularly grueling week—perhaps homecoming or exam week—this type of teacher may feel that his students deserve a much-needed rest. He may even declare a study hall or suggest a party. Or, because a holiday or summer vacation is imminent, he imbibes the holiday spirit and joins his only-too-willing students by celebrating early. This teacher, to use the jargon of our day, likes to party.

Other teachers are stronger-willed. But although they may hold out longer, eventually they capitulate. Their students know that if they whine, fuss and cajole long enough, their efforts will be rewarded; they will win a respite from schoolwork.

Pressure to coast assails teachers under various guises. Students may pressure teachers to relax by duping them into thinking that they are unusual. "None of the *other* teachers are making us work today," is a favorite line. Inexperienced teachers, especially, may lack the fortitude to respond with something like, "Yes, but I'm not just any teacher."

Another preferred ploy of savvy students is to appeal to the teacher's sense of closure. Since most of us are reluctant to launch into a new unit of study only to have it interrupted with a holiday, we tend to postpone it and coast a day or two. Other teachers complete the entire prescribed curriculum with a week or so remaining, then fritter away the rest of the school year rather than use it for review or enrichment.

A secondary teacher may coast when he falls into the shoddy habit of finishing his lesson with a few minutes left before the bell rings. Instead of reviewing the day's lesson or previewing tomorrow's, he kicks back and allows the class to "pack up" and talk quietly. He fails to realize that those lost minutes soon add up to lost hours and days and may translate into lower achievement-test scores.

Now only a teacher with a sadistic bent would never allow his students a hiatus from schoolwork. Certainly class parties and such have their time and place. But some teachers seem to include relaxation as a regular part of their lesson plans! And that's where disciplinary problems begin. Unscheduled time almost always degenerates into a student-controlled affair. The teacher who puts his class on automatic pilot is asking for turbulence, because few students handle freedom well.

By keeping students meaningfully occupied at all times, the teacher spares himself much stress. Camp directors learn early that they dare not plan schedules that allow campers too much free time, and teachers should follow suit. Idleness leads to mischief.

This is the first I've ever heard of it

Mr. Stockton, a high-school history teacher and former football coach, prided himself in never having to bother the administration with student discipline problems. He knew administrators were swamped and, besides, that was one area he could handle by himself.

Until Chad.

Admitted on probation in late September, Chad took it upon himself to drive Mr. Stockton into early retirement. A deceitful boy with a checkered record, Chad bragged to his classmates about his success in driving other teachers to distraction in other schools. As if on a mission, Chad set about to make life miserable for Mr. Stockton. Finally, after weeks of class showdowns and a mutual distaste for each other that was evident to the entire class, the time bomb exploded. After Chad challenged Stockton in class one day over a seating reassignment, the teacher put his arm around Chad's shoulder, marched him down to the office, and announced defiantly to the startled principal, "Either *he* goes or *I* go!"

Mr. Stockton's mistake, the principal told him in a later conference, was that the principal had no inkling that any animosity existed between the two. This was the first time he had heard that Chad was a problem.

Other teachers may not be too proud to admit that they can't handle certain students, but they may be too timid. They don't want to burden the administration with their problems, and they may even believe their job would be jeopardized if they did. But the rub comes, with such thinking, when an exasperated teacher finally throws in the proverbial towel and blindsides the administration with an ultimatum like Mr. Stockton's. The humiliating aspect of this scenario is that few administrators would follow a teacher's recommendation, even though they may be sympathetic, if they had not been previously apprised of brewing trouble.

Frustrating as it may be, we live in an age of due process. The rules are different now. Though that may vex our righteous souls, it is unlikely that we will ever return to the good ol' days of swift Old Testament justice. So in all but isolated incidents of sufficient magnitude, we must be willing to build a case against an unruly student—to document, communicate and sometimes sit on our hands. Most Christian schools are willing to "cast out the scorner," but only if a case has been built. When the administration is forewarned, not kept in the dark, they will be much more willing to take action. And who knows, if the administration is brought into the case early enough, perhaps even a Chad can be salvaged. After all, none of us want to expel a student if he can be saved. Discipline problems can sometimes be avoided when others, beside the teacher, are helping to shoulder the burden.

The proud or timid teacher who attempts to leap tall buildings in a single bound—to handle all festering discipline problems himself—is not facing reality. Today it takes more than the teacher; the administration must also be kept informed and involved.

Captivating Your Audience

Someone has quipped, "Yawning may be bad manners or just an honest opinion." We chuckle at that, but to the student assigned to a ho-hum teacher, it is no laughing matter. He is stuck with that teacher for nine months, so out of frustration he desperately seeks to occupy his mind in other ways.

Boredom will spawn misbehavior more quickly than almost anything. School administrators, consequently, have a low tolerance for boring teachers. I once knew an administrator in charge of keeping order in his Christian school. When certain less-than-exciting teachers would send him students who "refused to pay attention," as they put it, he would usually be lenient with the alleged perpetrators. He knew that captivated students rarely cause problems, and rather than mete out the justice the teacher deemed necessary—often a punishment bordering on flogging—this administrator felt more compelled to congratulate the child for not dropping out of school altogether! He knew that in a couple of classrooms the teachers lacked sparkle.

Surveys of school administrators conducted by the American Association of School Administrators and other similar groups, have discovered that the root causes of most disciplinary infractions are student apathy and lack of motivation.

Similarly, church research has shown that most kids who abandon Sunday school do so out of boredom. The teacher who is unable to generate some degree of excitement for learning will have students who are easily distracted by something more enticing.

Keep the show moving!

One of the best ways to ward off the classroom doldrums is to maintain a lively teaching pace. The Apostle Paul plainly tells us that whatever we do for the Lord we should do heartily (Colossians 3:23). We are not suggesting a kind of frenzy like that of the BBC sportscaster who got so excited at games that he became incoherent and finally had to resign! Rather, we are talking about a controlled enthusiasm that is infectious. The word *enthusiasm* is a derivative of a Greek word that literally means *God in you*, and is, thus, most appropriate for Christian school-teachers.

Students prefer teachers who seize the moment instantly once the bell rings. A teacher lost in his roll book in those first crucial seconds has lost the initiative by default. If the *teacher* seemingly does not know what to do next, the *students* surely do!

Students like teachers who set time limits. One of the best teachers I've ever known was a lady who set time limits for practically every directive ("You've got eight seconds to pass your papers forward....In two minutes, I'm going to call on someone to tell me the recurring theme of this poem"). Even high-schoolers like the challenge of beating the clock. When a teacher keeps the show moving, few students are tempted by distractions and no one nods off.

Students like a classroom in which there is little *dead air*. One dread of every radio or television station manager is that unplanned pause when nothing is being broadcast. They know that the audience will quickly tune to another station that *is* broadcasting, especially in this age of remote controls when most of us have the attention span of a gerbil. The same holds true for the classroom. The teacher who punctuates his teaching with dead air—who puts his class on mental hold—will find his students tuning him out and tuning in something else.

Dead air takes several forms and can result from any teacher who:

- Allows too much transition time between activities.
- Overstates his answer to a student's question.
- Has no back-up activity ready in case the projector bulb dies.
- Simply talks too slowly.

The teacher who laboriously phrases each sentence—like an attorney carefully choosing his words—will have students who mentally sprint ahead of him. The average person talks at the rate of 125 words per minute, but the average hearer can comprehend 1000 words per minute. Although this does not mean that the teacher must race through his lesson, it does mean that if he drones on at 16 RPM he will engender mental drift in his students.

Handling Troublemakers Quickly, Calmly, Inconspicuously

In order to maintain the interest of the class, a teacher must not dwell on discipline. Certainly not to be overlooked, of course, misbehavior must be downplayed and treated matter-of-factly as much as possible. By dealing with class disturbances quickly, calmly and—if feasible—inconspicuously, a teacher signals to the misbehaving student and the class as a whole, that such conduct gets a rise out of no one. Some kids will try a teacher's every "button," just to see what kind of response they get. If they evoke little response, they will stop pushing buttons. But if the teacher spends too much time in quelling eruptions, the class will soon cue in on the unspoken message that the way to sidetrack the teacher and draw attention to themselves is to misbehave. They will learn that that button can even postpone a test and may occasionally come in handy.

Discipline should be handled quickly, as it occurs. Ecclesiastes 8:11 recommends that, whenever possible, justice should be executed speedily. The teacher who has to pause too long to ponder his response to each infraction may have already lost the skirmish. No errant student should be allowed to monopolize class time in this way. In most cases, teachers must react promptly because, as one Christian school principal put it, "You must be on top of everything or the students will be on top of *you!*"

Discipline should be handled calmly. A teacher who argues, fusses, nags, rants and raves risks open warfare with his class. There is a high probability that he will play right into their hands and be forced to resort to questionable methods of restoring order. A teacher may be irked, but he must control himself to the point where he does not show it. Some teachers are able to develop an effective nonchalance about misconduct, deftly incorporating the name of the disobedient child into their lecture without missing a beat: "So we see, Tommy, that the main reason the South lost the Civil War was because…."

Whenever feasible, discipline should be handled inconspicuously. A class is sometimes like an irritable baby. Once the teacher is able to calm the baby, he should place a "do not disturb" sign on his desk to remind himself not to *wake the baby*. Some teachers set the class to working contentedly on seatwork only to unwittingly shatter the tranquillity by suddenly interrupting this cherished silence with further instructions. Other teachers *wake* the entire class when handling one student's minor infraction. The student may have been talking to a neighbor, but the teacher draws everyone's attention to the incident by calling out the student's name rather than silently motioning to the student. Such teachers have not learned that it is best to draw students aside and deal with minor infractions in such situations with firm-but-whispered tones. Just as we would try to avoid confronting an angry parent in the school's front office, in full view of others, so teachers should do all they can not to attract the attention of the entire class when handling just one or two individuals.

These are the rules

It is only reasonable to spell out the rules and punishments at the outset of the school year. Research indicates that if students can be involved in the creation of such a code, at least to some degree, they will feel more ownership and will more readily comply.

But this recommendation goes further. Teachers must give students clear limitations *any*time they expect specific results. That includes how to lay out a research paper, how to behave on a field trip or how to construct a science project. Some teachers are notorious for their foggy directions and penalizing students unable to read their mind.

"He who is soon angry dealeth foolishly"

When it comes to handling discipline, the teacher must keep a cool head. This is easier said than done, especially after a long day of corralling a class full of demanding children; but with the Lord's enabling, it is possible to get the victory.

He who cannot control his emotions, says Solomon, is as vulnerable as an unwalled city (Proverbs 25:28). Asking a teacher to keep a rein on his temper is a reasonable requisite of the profession. There are enough situations that arise daily to test a teacher that if he lacks self-control, it will soon be evident to all. An *unwalled* teacher exposes himself in diverse ways.

- Imposing new disciplinary standards without allowing any acclimation time.
- Demanding that a child act like an adult.
- Never compromising.
- Taking delight in making the course so difficult that students rarely experience success.
- Overdoing punishment.
- Punishing the entire class for the sins of a few. This often leads students to figure: Since all will be punished anyway, all might as well enjoy the sin.
- Demanding restitution before a student has simmered down.
- Making a "federal case" out of a minor infraction.
- Handing down a verdict before hearing both sides.

The teacher with a short fuse will find himself singed by his own explosions. His anger will only evoke backlash from his students and, thus, a vicious circle is born. The teacher who is prone to "soon anger" will make foolish judgments, hastening his eventual downfall.

CHAPTER SEVEN

DEVELOPING A STUDENT
LEADERSHIP STRATEGY

"If every teacher would take on a yearlong project of mentoring a single student, we would see a tremendous wave of new leadership emerge in our schools."
—**Dan L. Burrell, Ed.D.**

Traditionally, educators give much lip service to the goal of training future leadership as part of our educational mission. There are times when we look across the classroom or down the class roster and break into a cold sweat with the realization that these kids will at some point in the future be responsible for deciding whether or not we receive social security. And we don't even want to consider the whole euthanasia debate. But those who have ministered in Christian education for any length of time also know the joys that come as we observe our students maturing into leaders who take up important roles in their homes, our churches and our communities.

Several years ago I actually had my former principal working for me (albeit briefly) in our school as a classroom teacher. More recently, I have hired several of my former students as teachers. Currently I am having one sharp young former student bring me even further into the information and technology age. I looked at him recently and plaintively exclaimed, "Eddie, I can't believe that you are teaching me now when every time that I look at you, I see an ornery twelve-year-old that consistently made my life very interesting." But it is extremely rewarding to see those "ornery" young men and women mature into outstanding leaders. We can facilitate this process as we give attention to several aspects of developing student leadership.

I can't tell you that I have ever observed a specific strategy for the development of leadership functioning in a school setting. However, I have seen components in numerous schools that consistently produce young men and women of initiative and character. It is these components that I wish to outline here and add a few personal suggestions for their implementation in the traditional school setting.

Most behavioral psychologists and educators will tell you that natural leadership skills are observable in the earliest years of the education process. As you observe preschoolers on the playground, you will quickly notice that a *pecking order* rapidly forms. There will be several *mother hens* trying to organize and direct. There will be *roosters* perched on the playground equipment, crowing and shouting. A few loners will drift to the edges of the play area and discreetly pick at the out-of-the-way objects that capture their attention.

However, the type of leadership we want to see develop is twofold. The first type is the natural leadership that is a part of the makeup and personality of some. These leaders are the ones who thrive when they are in charge, in public and in power. They want to be line leaders, class officers, team captains and spokespeople. They have a mission in life and that mission is to be in front and to influence. This leadership does not require development as much as it needs channeling. These young people can be intimidating and frustrating. They are often opinionated and headstrong. Research will also show that many of these young people are first-born and more often than not, male.

The second type of leadership we want to develop is that of individual character. Every student should develop a sense of him or herself that gives them the confidence to act on their convictions through the strength of their character. There are multiple characteristics of this type of leadership, including initiative, self-esteem, independence, loyalty, courage and perseverance. Not every student is born to be president, but each can develop a level of personal leadership that will help him or her live lives of strength and Christian character.

Here are some of the components which, when implemented in a school setting, can help students develop Christian leadership.

Reward the right behaviors

In many classrooms, the student who receives the most attention is the one who creates the greatest commotion. This is done by demonstrating out-of-the-norm behavior, and much of it is usually negative. Most of us can look back on our childhood experiences and remember two particular students—the class *clown* and the class *jock*. The class clown was the one who always made us laugh. He was always "on the edge" with the teacher and yet, interestingly enough, even the teacher would find him amusing on occasion. Quick-witted and popular, this student would often care little about academics or accomplishments, not to mention the feelings of the unfortunate foils of his humor. Regardless of his lack of ambition, he commonly received accolades for the fact that he was a party-in-progress. The class jock was always the slightly-more-mature-than-the-rest athlete who excelled by virtue of physical prowess and often appearance. She was the perky captain of the cheerleading squad. He was the cool football hero. Everyone knew that there were few higher positions in life than to sit at the same cafeteria table as the jocks.

No one plans this kind of "leadership" among the students; it just happens. But all too frequently, even the teachers get caught up in it. They call attention to the exploits of the athletes as illustrations in class. They smirk at the latest remark of the clown, much to the delight of the students. When a general question is asked, without even considering what they are doing, the teacher gravitates toward these "leaders" for a response.

At the back of the class, however, is a quiet girl with thick glasses and a weight problem. To her left is an awkwardly skinny fellow who has severe acne. No one can tell it now, but there is incredible potential hidden in their cores. In fact, some of the "tough" lessons they learn at the bottom of the schoolyard pecking order will give them the character and skills to succeed in a different community years down the road. A flicker of attention from the teacher would make their day. To be recognized for some achievement or behavior would be the source of a life-long memory. The wise educator looks for the leadership of character in *every* student.

Instead of noting the accomplishments of last Friday's stellar performance on the ball field, how about making note of the person who stands up for other students when they are being teased or ridiculed. Call attention to personal neatness. Recognize quick obedience. Ask the overlooked student to do a special favor. Assign a leadership opportunity to the "less-than-perfect" student. Call on the quiet student who sits in the back.

Among the qualities that we should recognize are obedience, punctuality, initiative, hard work, perseverance, faithfulness, compassion, friendliness, helpfulness and dependability. Talent is never a substitute for character. You can borrow brains, but you can't borrow character. Perhaps by only recognizing athletics, talents and academics, we miss out on rewarding the best behaviors and reduce our kids to a performance-based mentality that emphasizes the wrong things.

Last year I had my assistant design a sticker that says: "I got caught doing good by the Pastor!" She ordered a role of them from the local Insty-Prints. I carry a few of these in my pocket, and when I catch a student holding a door open for a teacher, picking up trash or some other demonstration of personal character, I stick one on their uniform like a badge of honor. The student may then give it to the clerk at the cafeteria and receive a free ice cream. By rewarding good behavior, I hope to see it repeated and to encourage the development of student leadership.

Promote leadership training

There are numerous organizations in place that will assist you with leadership training. The American Association of Christian Schools offers an extensive schedule of Student Leadership Conferences for the training of select students on a secondary level. Traditional venues of leadership training, such as National Honor Society and Boy's and Girl's State, may also be considered. Summit Ministries in Colorado offers outstanding programs from a Christian perspective for student leaders and education leaders on the development of a Christian worldview.

You can promote participation in these opportunities in several ways:

- Offer scholarships for students with potential.
- Encompass a leadership retreat or seminar with a class trip.
- Hold a leadership retreat prior to the start of the school year.
- Look for retreats scheduled at Christmas and spring break.

Emphasize activities that build long-term, practical leadership

Most schools set up athletic programs early in their existence. Large sums of capital are invested in these programs, and they are among the most popular and demanded extracurricular activities that we offer. Yet, how many of our schools have produced a single professional athlete? (And if we have, are we proud of that fact?)

There are few programs that will develop more practical, long-term leadership skills than the fine arts program. We speak in cliché-like terms of "developing tomorrow's church leaders today." However, in terms of resource assignments, we seem more intent on "developing tomorrow's armchair quarterbacks today."

In reality, the child who learns to sing, give a speech, play an instrument or teach a lesson will have a skill that will last beyond the "athletic" years and which can be utilized in the local church for an entire lifetime. Long after the muscles have atrophied and the weight has redistributed itself around our midriffs, we can be having an affect on eternity by singing in church choirs, preaching from pulpits, teaching Sunday school and working as missionaries.

There is much that can be learned on the ball field, and I'm not suggesting that athletic programs be discontinued. I do believe we should revisit our program and budgetary priorities and reconsider the attention we give to the development of leadership skills that can be used in service to the Lord. More attention needs to be directed toward the utilization of leadership skills in the local church, which will have the greatest impact on eternity.

Mentoring enhances leadership

While I am sometimes accused of sounding like a broken record on this topic, personal discipleship of young people will do more for the development of leadership than any school-wide program. When Paul needed to train a "young preacher," how did he do it? He mentored an immature whippersnapper by the name of Timothy. His counsel included: "Let no man despise thy youth; but be thou an example of the believers…" (1 Timothy 4:12). His letters to Timothy are part of the scriptural record and an outstanding example of the impact of spiritual mentorship.

If every teacher would take on a yearlong project of mentoring a single student, we would see a tremendous wave of new leadership emerge in our schools. These relationships would be of immeasurable benefit and significance to the student. In addition, the teachers would find an exciting encouragement in this type of relationship. It is altogether possible to develop this type of interaction without crossing the boundaries of appropriate student-teacher relationships. In fact, for many years, major colleges and universities, such as Harvard and Georgetown, had mentorship programs in place, which assigned a professor to a student for just such a purpose.

Teach social and decorum skills

Students who become leaders will have frequent interaction with adults and in adult social settings. One of the reasons some students avoid leadership is that they are intimidated by the protocol of the adult world. We do our students a great service by teaching them how to behave in such settings. There are few experiences more uncomfortable to an adolescent than *sticking out* in unfamiliar surroundings.

Here is a list of skills that will give your students confidence in adult social and leadership settings once they are mastered.

- How to introduce yourself to a stranger.
- How to shake hands with a member of the opposite sex.
- How to introduce others to someone of higher rank.
- How to seat a lady or be seated by a gentleman.
- How to eat at a formal dinner.
- How to dress for a formal function.
- How to seek an appointment/interview.
- How to follow-up on an appointment/interview.
- How to make a favorable impression.
- How to engage and sustain someone in conversation appropriately.
- How to treat those that are older/younger than you.

These skills can be taught as part of a Christian manhood or ladies finishing class. Skills in these areas will give our students an *edge* in social and leadership settings and will give them confidence. Society appreciates a poised and confident young person who is articulate and considerate.

Encourage student initiatives

Because of the disciplined environment of many Christian school classrooms and campuses, we may be unintentionally squelching individual initiatives from students who have leadership potential. By maintaining absolute control on seniors, we may have made a wrong assessment as to their ability to make good independent decisions. By requiring that all initiatives be faculty or administration lead, we may be missing a tremendous opportunity to see the creative leadership of our charges in action.

Through student government, school clubs and participation in community outreach activities, the students can find avenues for expression in leadership. Remember that the students will not always do things *exactly* as you would do them. But if you will give them space, you may actually find that they will, on occasion, do them better! We do our students no service by preventing them from experiencing mistakes and even failure. Sometimes the wise teacher will step back and let an excited student with a leadership initiative flutter about like a confused nestling; but eventually they will soar away with success. It is important that the older student, who is of a strong will and possesses a spirit of leadership, receives understanding and guidance from his instructors. Too often teachers mistake a strong will for a rebellious spirit. An aggressive teenage young man who is misunderstood by a teacher can develop a rebellious, angry response. We must teach the students to submit to authority without robbing them of their leadership desires or the strong spirit that will propel them into positions of influence in the future.

Student leadership is one of the most important aspects of a good Christian education. Someday the leaders we train may actually become the leaders we serve. With that in mind, let us develop the kind of leaders that have the godly character and personal qualities that will serve them and us well.

CHAPTER EIGHT

PARENT-TEACHER CONFERENCES

"If nothing else, we have one very important thing in common with all of our students' parents: We both love their child."
—**Philip C. Johnson, Ph.D.**

What is it about the parent-teacher conference that makes the hair on the back of our necks stand up and causes us to want to run and hide? Most of us are fairly familiar with parents in general. We've all *had* parents; some of us *are* parents; most have *known* people who have parents; or, at the very least, you've read an article about parents. And yet when it comes to the parents of the students we teach, we don't always know what to do with them.

Through the years, the relationship between parents and teachers has changed. There was a time, 50 or so years ago, when the "almighty" teachers were never questioned. They were revered and perhaps a little feared, even by parents. Those days are gone. The pendulum has swung so far in the other direction now that many teachers feel they can never win what is perceived as the parent-teacher conflict. The result is paranoia regarding parent relationships. This is unfortunate, because it is really a very small percentage of parents who have made many teachers feel this way. This pervasive feeling has resulted in a basic lack of trust on both sides of the fence. The teacher believes that the parent is bound to be uncooperative and accusatory; the parent often thinks that the teacher is difficult and secretive.

While some would rather avoid any and all contact with parents at any cost, others tramp right in and end up making enemies out of the very people we are in business to serve. The first thing that we, as educators, need to remember is that if nothing else, we have one very important thing in common with all of our students' parents: We both love their child. Parents need to be seen as allies, and the sooner we readjust our thinking regarding parents and our relationship with parents, the sooner we will see more success in our conferences. We do not need to harbor an us-versus-them mindset but rather the mentality of teamwork. We both ought to have the same goal: the spiritual, social and academic success of their child.

The Relationship

Establishing proper parent relationships is the cornerstone to successful future conferences. The sooner we turn parents into allies, the sooner we will gain their support when we are faced with challenges in the classroom (usually challenges generated by their child). Here are some principles to follow that will help to set the stage for future confrontation.

Cultivate a positive relationship with parents from the beginning

The time to build a relationship with anyone is before there are problems. As a general rule, the period of trouble-free time that you will experience with a student, from the time you meet them until the time it becomes necessary to meet with their parents, is about 12 minutes. So don't be shy; move quickly in building your positive relationship.

It is the wise teacher who understands that a child is an extension of the parents' egos. Often this child that will be placed in your care is the embodiment of all the hopes and unfulfilled dreams of their parents. Therefore, when you need to share something negative about that child with his or her parents, it affects those parents on a very personal level. While you may be able to feel terribly objective about the fact that Billy spit in Martha's milk carton and then laughed as she drank it, Mom and Dad won't be quite so detached. They will probably feel that you have just accused them of spitting in Martha's milk, and a plethora of conflicting feelings are sure to follow. This is why it is so important to lay as much positive groundwork as early as possible. You want to convey to parents in an honest and frequent way that you love their child. Building this foundation of security will allow the relationship to hold up when more negative meetings are necessary.

There are many ways to accomplish this, but one of the easiest ways is to simply pick up the telephone, call a parent and share something positive about their child. I can promise you that this will not take very much time out of your evening. First of all, when the parent hears your voice they will be expecting some horrific news. When they realize that you've called to tell them something *good* about their child, the effect will be something akin to that of a stun gun and will allow you to make a quick and clean getaway. You're in, you're out—no one gets hurt. The final result: You've encouraged a child and a parent and made it easier for yourself in the event you ever need to share negative information in the future.

Communicate often

Don't allow the first nine weeks of school to go by before you communicate with parents. They should hear from you in the form of a card, letter or phone call within the first week of school. If you need to, make yourself a schedule so that you will have some accounting of regular communication with parents. In this way, when there is the hint of a problem, parents can be made aware of the situation before it turns into something like grand theft auto. I believe that one of the biggest frustrations plaguing parents is not knowing about a problem early enough to correct it in a timely fashion. And one of the most unpleasant statements a teacher can hear from a parent is: "Why am I just hearing about this problem now?"

There's really no good answer to this unless you're brave enough to say, "Well, Mrs. Mason, we all had a big meeting and thought it would be a whole lot of fun to keep this situation from you until it developed into something really alarming." And then you can see how fast you can make it down to the unemployment office. Frequent communication will save you from many intensely awkward conversations and meetings later.

Documentation

Save things; don't get caught sharing information with parents that you can't back up with paperwork. And it is always preferable to have documents that have the parent's signature on them. This is true regarding graded papers, detention slips, behavioral forms and late homework assignments. This will save you lots of time and headaches during any conference when someone might intimate that they were not aware of Nancy's poor grades. In a very kind and tactful way you can produce the poor grades that were signed by the parents. Now let me warn you: As tempting and as fun as it might be in this situation, don't gloat. It's just not right, at least not until the parent has left your room (just kidding!). The point is this: Be prepared! We all know the satisfaction of presenting a well-prepared case, and we all know what happens when we can't back up our claims. Prepare yourself by implementing a system of careful documentation. The goal is simply to get the student back on track as quickly as possible.

The Conference

Face it: Junior's going to mess up sooner or later. There will come that day when you will ask Mr. and/or Mrs. Smith to come in and see you. Or it is possible that Mr. and Mrs. Smith might have heard about one of your classroom activities that went awry and will want to make an appointment with you. It doesn't really matter when, why or how; you *will* be meeting with them. Here are some strategies that might help you as you wander through the minefield commonly known as the parent-teacher conference.

Open the conference in prayer

Try having the *parent* open the meeting in prayer. I guarantee you that they won't be expecting this; but the purpose of this is not just the element of surprise, though that does have its own benefits. Having parents lead in prayer is valuable because it prompts parents to understand right up front that relying on spiritual wisdom is vital to the success of the conference. I have also seen this effectively and quickly change parental attitudes. It is hard to stay mad, defensive or just plain cranky when entering the throne room of God. It's your conference; you have the right to establish the proper spiritual atmosphere. But don't force the issue. If the parent isn't willing to open in prayer, then you just go right ahead and do it yourself.

Don't be defensive

When you meet parents for a conference, be warm and friendly; be confident. If you've kept up good communication and kept good records, then you have every reason to believe that this conference will proceed in a successful manner. (If you haven't done all of those things, then you might try bursting into tears and going for the sympathy ploy…whatever you feel comfortable with.)

Whatever you do, don't be defensive. As a former administrator, the number one complaint that I would hear from parents regarding communication with teachers was that the teacher would get defensive. I believe that is often the case. We are so concerned with protecting ourselves, that we don't take time to listen to parents. Most parents will come to you with a genuine concern for helping you get their child over a rough spot. Occasionally a parent will cause you to feel backed into a corner and, like a caged animal, you just might feel like biting. Mentally and spiritually prepare yourself prior to the conference and determine that you will remain in control of yourself and your emotions. Being defensive will make you appear guilty and argumentative and will certainly not be glorifying to the Lord.

You also do not need to feel intimidated. This is a common feeling among many teachers. An angry parent will come in and begin slinging their bouquets of accusations at you, and you are bound to feel a bit overwhelmed. You begin stuttering, mumbling, shaking; the whole thing is just not pretty. Remember that God is not a God of fear.

Take time to listen to what the parent is saying. Don't try to refute what the parent is saying, just let them spew and get it out of their systems. This also gives you time to gain your composure (or to make mental grocery lists). Just wait out the storm.

Usually when people are upset, their anger will feed off the other person's reactions. It's kind of hard to keep an argument going when there's only one person doing the arguing. This is one of the benefits associated with being quiet; and most people look smarter when their mouth is closed anyway. It is really no fun at all to argue with someone who will not argue back. When there is a break in the storm, use the opportunity to apply the biblical injunction: "A soft answer turneth away wrath..."(Proverbs 15:1).

Every now and again you might get a parent who is just really out of control. In a situation like this, you need to firmly and politely share with the parent that you would be happy to sit down and have a conference with them when they are under control. Then leave. Do not allow yourself to be drawn into an argument or a shouting match. Notify your supervisor of the situation and then commit it into God's sovereign hands and get a good night's sleep.

Get to the point

Sometimes because of the awkwardness of a conference, a teacher may feel compelled to make small talk. This is usually not necessary. Both you and the parent know that you are there for a specific purpose, and usually the parent is very anxious to hear about the situation that has caused them to have to be sitting in your classroom or office. After a pleasant greeting and opening in prayer, get directly to the point. Parents appreciate professional straightforwardness. There is no reason to apologize for having scheduled the conference. There is no reason to apologize for the situation. Simply and kindly relate the matter at hand and begin working on a solution with the parent. They will appreciate the professional manner, and it will make the conference much easier for everyone involved.

End with something positive

After you have completed the conference and shared what had to be shared, make sure that you don't leave the parent with a feeling of hopelessness. Let the parent know that you love their child and are looking forward to and expecting improvement from their child. Teachers do not always know everything that is going on in the parent's or child's home life. As far as the parent is concerned, this conference could be just about the last straw in a long line of problems they've been experiencing. Parents need to understand that you view the problem as totally solvable if the proper effort from the student and support from home is applied.

What if you are in the wrong?

A conference for which you are totally prepared is unnerving enough. If that is not enough of a thrill for you, try going into a conference that is occurring because you have really blown it. If nothing else, this will cause you to understand the value of a really good deodorant. What do you do in a conference situation when there is no possible way to win, mainly because *you* are the one who messed up? Perhaps you forgot that note in Jack's permanent record that stated that he was "bladder-control challenged." So you denied him his tenth trip to the restroom for the day and the result was embarrassing for everyone. Maybe Jane had a detention slapped on her in a moment when you thought you had all of the facts, only to find out *after* she served the detention, that it was really Mary who had propelled the monster spit wad into the left ear of Billy. Most of us would rather never be in these types of situations, but we're human and it's going to happen. So what do you do? I've found that the best tactic is to simply say, "I'm sorry."

We live in a world where everyone constantly tries to cover their tracks so fast and so often that parents will come to you *expecting* you to offer excuses. But if you've messed up, you've messed up. There's really no way around it. Just admit it, apologize sincerely, and do what you can to make the situation right. Then go to the student and apologize to him or her. You will be surprised with the response that you get. This is also a perfect opportunity for your parents and students to see you for what you are—for what all of us are: sinners saved by God's grace. We're not perfect just because we're Christians, but we are striving to grow more like Christ each day. What a great opportunity to teach your students how to be humble, to ask for forgiveness and to get back to the business of growing.

As educators, our ministry is people, and that includes the parents of our students. Parents have entrusted their most precious possession to us—their child. Take the fear out of parent-teacher conferences by taking the time and making the effort to develop healthy and positive relationships with parents. This will make it possible for us to be their allies in helping their children wade through the rough waters of growing up and growing in Christ.

CHAPTER NINE

WINNING PARENTS
THROUGH INVOLVEMENT

"The more parents are involved in their child's school,…the more supportive they are apt to be."

—Paul Tatham

"I'd like to help in Mr. Smitherton's class," announced a parent as she entered the school office. "I've wanted to get involved in Becky's class for some time, and now that my work hours have been rearranged, I think I can swing it."

I made some lame excuse along the lines of the class likely not needing help, thanks very much anyway, knowing that Smitherton was not at the top of our showcase-teachers list. As principal, I had observed Smitherton on several occasions and had come to the conclusion that he was "a work in progress." But Becky's mom was determined.

"Oh I'm sure Mr. Smitherton can use me *somewhere*," she insisted. "I know he has a ton of papers to grade, and I've *seen* his bulletin boards." Not taking my hint, I relented and arranged for Becky's mom to help in the classroom every Tuesday morning. "We'll soon be losing that family," I mumbled to my secretary after the mother left. Knowing Smitherton, I was sure that once his new parent-volunteer experienced his classroom firsthand, she would bail…with Becky in tow.

Becky's mom came faithfully every Tuesday, but it took me several weeks before I could muster enough courage to ask her how things were going.

"Just great!" she replied with a beaming smile. I tried not to show my surprise. "He's got me doing all kinds of things with those kids." I couldn't believe it. I was sure we had lost a good family, eager to complete their withdrawal slip after the first week of observing Smitherton in action. I was wrong.

After inquiring of other Christian school principals and researching through old college textbooks, I stumbled upon an educational principle I had long forgotten; the fact that the more parents are involved in their child's school, the more supportive they are apt to be. Even if the teacher they are assisting is not teacher-of-the-year caliber.

One would think just the opposite would be true. If I allow parents to get too close to our staff, we might imagine they would soon discover that some teachers have feet of clay! Then they'd spread the word to everyone else! Their confidence in us would be undermined! All kinds of false fears race through our minds in such situations.

Instead, involved parents invariably jump to the other side and become our staunchest allies. "I don't know how that lady does it," one parent told me recently, after helping her child's class with several projects. "She's amazing! I could never do her job all day. In fact, I've added her to my prayer list!"

Wise principals know what every pastor knows intuitively: If you want supportive parishioners, involve them. Someone doesn't like the music? Encourage her to join the choir. Criticizes the Sunday school? Offer him a class. Complains about unruly AWANA kids? Put him on a visitation team. The same principle works its magic in Christian schools.

Putting out the welcome mat

With that in mind, the prudent principal encourages his school board and staff to adopt a there's-a-welcome-here mentality. After all, if we aren't proud of what we do, perhaps we shouldn't be doing it. Admittedly, we aren't perfect, but no organization is. We know we have flaws, and if we pretend we don't, everyone will quickly see through our charade anyway. Or as John succinctly put it: "If we say that we have no sin, we deceive ourselves..." (1 John 1:8).

Many parents hardly need a welcome; they come to us eager to be involved. They may have transferred from a non-Christian school where, perhaps, they felt welcomed yet philosophically aloof. Especially our parents who know Christ as Savior understand that the biblical caution—concerning the difficulty of two walking together except they be agreed—may have applied to their previous school experience. Now that these parents have enrolled in a Christian school, however, they come to us already leaning in our direction. The values and beliefs we teach are their values and beliefs; our aspirations for the students are akin to theirs; our methodologies dovetail with their expectations. Since we often begin on common ground, a partnership is forged from the outset. They come to support us, not subvert us.

Christian-school administrators rarely have to persuade applying parents about the benefits of well-behaved classes, challenging academics, biblically-based curricula or civilized playmates. Most new parents already understand and support what we seek to accomplish. A bond, a rapport, exists before the admissions process is even initiated.

Such a natural affinity makes long-term success all the more probable, leaving the Christian school only to maintain the momentum.

Maintaining the momentum

The Christian school can further build upon that natural bond in a variety of ways. Opportunities for parental involvement are seemingly endless, so we will explore only a few.

It begins by communicating to parents that their involvement is, indeed, welcome. We cannot assume that parents automatically understand this posture, for they may have come from another school where they were kept at arm's length. The student-parent manual, the admissions interview, parent orientation night and class bulletins should all send a similar message: We want you! Once that welcome is articulated, it is time to give parents some specifics. OK, you've sold me. I'm convinced. Now, where do I sign up?

Parent orientation night

For many parents, involvement in their child's school begins with an introductory briefing called a *parent orientation* night. Held within the first week or two of each school year, this meeting acquaints parents with the school and the opportunities for involvement that it promises.

Although the drawing card is a portion of the evening set aside for parents to visit their child's classroom, sit in his desk and meet his teachers, the meeting presents an ideal opportunity for schools to interest parents in exciting opportunities for deeper involvement. This is the time to capture their interest. It's a new year, and everyone is fresh and eager. When the evening is over, parents are always enthusiastic and optimistic. They are more familiar with the inner workings of their child's classroom and school and, hence, more likely to support it.

Room mothers

An age-old form of parental involvement is that of room mothers. Reserved primarily for the elementary grades, room mothers are volunteers who assist with class parties, field trips and the like. The appeal for such volunteers is often made at a get-acquainted program that marks a new school year. Invariably, teachers find that more than enough mothers are eager for such service, and that their help can be invaluable throughout the year.

As an administrator, I have dropped in on many classroom functions and commented on the elaborate culinary spread or beautifully decorated displays. More often than not, the teacher will whisper in my ear, "The room mothers did the whole thing. I didn't have to do anything. They're fantastic!"

Productions

Parents love to be involved in student productions of all descriptions. Perhaps it is because they remember the thrill they themselves felt when they were in school, or perhaps they simply want to be part of a production that involves their child; but whatever the reason, soliciting parental support is not difficult. The occasion could be a talent show, a music concert or a drama production. Parents can be used as musical accompanists, publicists, ticketsellers, prop builders, stagehands, whatever.

Speakers

Parents are often an untapped source of student enrichment. Representing a plethora of careers and experiences, they have only to be called upon as classroom speakers, chapel speakers, seminar leaders and inservice contributors.

If used, such parents should be apprised of the school's position on various issues and, of course, first cleared through the administration. One would not want a chapel speaker, for example, soapboxing over a biblical concern that the school seeks to avoid.

Parents who are called upon to share their area of expertise at school usually feel a special attachment to that school for years thereafter. They know that we appreciated them enough to use them, and it is not often that people are called upon to showcase their knowledge.

Parent-teacher fellowship

Many Christian schools have found that a parent-teacher fellowship (PTF) is a foundational way to involve parents. Such an organization will not only serve to cement relationships and bond parents closer to the school, but it can generate substantial funding for a wide variety of causes. In many schools, in fact, the PTF is viewed almost *exclusively* as a fundraising organization.

To forestall the danger of a PTF exceeding its original mandate and exerting pressure on a school's administration and board in matters of policy, a wise school will draft some sort of constitution that spells out the limits of its power. Christian schools welcome parental involvement and suggestions, but we must be wary lest we create an organization that oversteps its bounds. Most Christian-school administrators can cite at least one school where this has transpired.

Sparse attendance at PTF meetings is a common concern among schools. Its cause may be traced to the sad fact that in modern American society both parents work and are often tired at the end of the day. They do not welcome an evening out following a demanding day on the job. Evening church services across the nation, incidentally, face the same dilemma. The solution, however, might lie in the hands of the PTF program planner. The simple inclusion of the school children themselves in the program is usually the only draw a parent needs. Want a crowd? Feature the students.

Parent ambassadors

A parent-ambassadors group can be formed to encourage inquiring families and welcome newly enrolled ones. Some schools refer applicants to their list of satisfied customers—parents eager to share what the school and the Lord means to them. Or, taken a step further, such a group of salesmen can be tapped to prepare a get-acquainted tea for new parents.

Families new to a school often feel estranged. They may be new in town and have only a handful of friends, so a PR-savvy school can take advantage of this opportunity to extend the right hand of fellowship and exhibit Christian love. Many families have been won to Christ with just such a welcome.

Homework helpers

Homework is as much a part of the educational land-scape as multiplication tables, lunch thermoses, and #2 pencils. It is as inseparable from the learning process as pop quizzes, for to have a school without homework would be like teaching without a chalkboard; something inherently *schoolish* would be missing.

But homework has fallen on hard times. Because of the increased likelihood that the child comes from a single-parent family or lives in a home where both parents work, he may have little adult supervision and assistance with his homework. Stepping into the breach, some schools have organized parents and grandparents who are available and willing to make themselves accessible by telephone to help unravel, say, the mystery of fractions to puzzled Johnny.

All some kids need to finish their homework is a little prodding. The fact that some adult is going to phone and ask how they are doing is the only impetus they need to get the job done.

Prayer partners

Parents who know Christ and have a spiritual burden for the students and teachers may desire to be involved in a prayer ministry. They realize the significance of spiritual warfare and know that unseen beings are constantly vying for the very souls of our students. Because prayer is power-ful, the role of such partners in defeating Satan and his henchmen may be the determining factor in a school's suc-cess.

Perhaps unseen and unappreciated, their ministry is vital nonetheless. Prayer is the common currency of *new* Chris-tian schools—schools in the conception stage—but too of-ten we seem to no longer need the Lord once we are established. We seem to forget that Satan is as determined to undermine our ministry when it is twenty years old as when it was first being considered.

A group of prayer partners can be formed and meet either at school or in homes, often on a weekly basis. They usually need little supervision on the part of the administration, and often all that is asked by such a group is an occasional list of prayer needs.

Some school prayer groups have developed a soul-winning ministry. Perhaps as a byproduct of their intercession, which often includes the souls of young people, the Lord has constrained them to get off their knees and into the hallways. Even in Christian schools, there is a mission field of lost souls that are ripe unto harvest, and all that is needed to bring them into the kingdom is someone concerned enough to ask about their spiritual state.

Sounding boards

A more casual form of parent involvement is that of an advisory council. This is a loosely knit group of parents that meets informally, either on a regular basis or at the principal's behest, so that he may seek their advice about proposals or simply ascertain the overall pulse of the parents.

This form of feedback is less conventional than the standard survey questionnaire, but it does serve to give the principal a glimpse into parental concerns. Perhaps meeting around coffee in a conference room, a relaxed handful of parents might be more prone to voice their ideas than if they were convened in a more formal "business" setting. Such groups, the makeup of which may be fluid, must realize that they carry no real power to change school policy. But we will want to convey to them that we seek their input, nonetheless, and are not intimidated by their suggestions.

Surveys

Surveys, touched upon in the previous section, are somewhat impersonal but still considered a form of parental involvement. Although the percentage of completed parent surveys that are returned to us may not always be as high as we would like, and it may seem that parents, as a whole, are a rather disinterested lot, it is safe to conclude that they do appreciate the gesture. Parents like to know that the school values their opinions.

The key to a higher return rate for surveys is directly correlated to their brevity. Parents are busy, and a survey that is cumbersome may be treated as just another piece of junk mail. Keep the questions brief, unambiguous and able to be answered with a few check marks. And never exceed more than one page.

Booster clubs

Booster clubs are parent organizations that support specific student groups—sports teams, music groups, drama groups, etc. Invariably, the parent's child is a member of the group, and the parent wants to play a contributory role in his child's enjoyment and the group's success. A wise school will capitalize on such parental interest.

Booster clubs serve primarily as fundraisers for their child's group, but they also enable parents to fellowship with other parents who share a common interest. Long-lasting friendships can develop, and boosters will often become a school's most spirited "cheerleaders" to those outside the school family.

Fundraisers

At first glance, to include fundraising as a form of parental involvement may seem like a stretch. But we are focusing our attention here on the solicitors, not on those being solicited.

Believe it or not, some parents actually *like* to ask others for money. Although most parents shy away from such crass forms of supplication, preferring instead more "respectable" types of involvement, there are some who are "born beggars" and seem to relish the opportunity to ask complete strangers to support good causes.

In one Christian school I administrated, our most ardent supporter was a mother who jumped at the opportunity to spearhead every fundraiser on the docket. She was such a diplomat and exuded such personal charm that she alone could be counted upon not only to enlist an army of volunteers but also ensure the drive's unquestioned success. When we turned over a fundraiser to this Heaven-sent saint, we could relax and simply wait for her praise reports.

Oddly enough, the more people this lady involved in fundraising with her, the more supportive of the school they became. Not one parent complained that they were being *used* in some way, thus validating the truism that the more parents are involved in a school, the more supportive they are apt to be...even if those parents are saddled with the unenviable task of soliciting funds.

Student trips

Having parents help chaperone student trips is a form of parent involvement. We are referring here to overnighters, not same-day field trips. Granted, not every trip is a winner. I have accompanied some parents who were overheard to mutter defiantly, "Never again!" at the conclusion of the trip. But such sour notes are rare. Most trips, though perhaps taxing, serve nonetheless to draw parents closer to the school. Parents bond with the students and other chaperones and seem to develop a new appreciation of what we are all about.

A school cannot ask just *any* parent to be a chaperone, of course. Selecting people who possess the right mix of law, grace and common sense cannot be taken lightly, for we want adults who can establish student rapport yet who are able to maintain school standards. Chaperones are arguably the single most important factor in the success of an overnight trip.

Trip rules must be clearly defined for the chaperones as much as for the students. The adults will want to know the school's expectations in areas such as dress code, restricted areas, boy-girl relationships, curfews, tardiness and attitudes. Veterans of such trips would advise us to have students and their parents sign a compliance form that spells out consequences for rule-breakers.

Visitation week

When parents are given an opportunity to get a taste of their child's daily school routine, they usually jump at the chance. Perhaps an entire week can be set aside, in order to accommodate as many parents as possible, when they are invited to sit in on classes. Parents themselves, in fact, may be willing to organize the whole affair. If nothing else, parents will appreciate the fact that their school has adopted a nothing-to-hide philosophy, especially appealing in this age of suspicion.

Parent coaches

The typical Christian school with an interscholastic athletic program scrambles to meet its coaching needs. One source to consider for assistant positions is the parents. There is a sizeable percentage of fathers and mothers out there who have the expertise, the time and the inclination to help. Many will offer their services *gratis*.

Such coaches, of course, will need to be screened and properly interviewed. They must be briefed as to their expected conduct, and they will have to be told—in a loving yet direct fashion—that they are not the *head* coach. Despite occasional obstacles and problems, such arrangements have usually proven beneficial to schools and have provided yet another means of bonding.

Parent volunteers

Because they are financially unable to provide adequate staffing, many Christian schools are forced to demand much of their employees. In contrast to their counterparts in public schools, and in some other private schools, many of our teachers are overworked. They work harder and are paid less. Though few complain, such conditions take their toll.

To alleviate the problem, give consideration to starting a formalized parent-volunteer program. Volunteerism, by definition, has no detrimental impact on a school's financial bottom line. The only expense involves the time of someone to coordinate the program, and some schools have even relegated that responsibility to a parent.

A parent volunteer program—in which parents come to school on a weekly basis to help in the classroom, library, office or wherever needed—provides the ultimate vehicle for parent involvement, if for no other reason than it involves regular, weekly contact between the home and school. Such programs have served to cultivate some of the strongest supporters any school could want.

Those who show interest in serving as volunteers should complete a brief application that asks, among other things, for areas in which they would like to serve; their days and hours of availability; and their willingness to comply with the school's standard of dress, conduct and doctrine. Included, too, should be a statement of moral integrity.

The ability to *keep* its volunteers is the true test of a program's success. Although there will always be some attrition, there are means a school can use to reduce that to a trickle. The quintessential way is so simple that it is often overlooked: appreciation. People will seek out places where they are appreciated. It's that simple. In fact, studies show that lack of appreciation is a leading reason why employees leave their jobs. Volunteers, though drawing no salary, will behave similarly.

Anything a school can do to show a volunteer how vital she is to the school's operations will go a long way toward fostering longevity. Appreciation may take the form of memos, letters from the board, phone calls, service plaques, recognition at parent gatherings or merely passing compliments in the hallway. Volunteers should be made to feel as much a part of the faculty family as possible.

Parent volunteerism is a double blessing. It can be an indispensable source of help for the harried teacher while, at the same time, bringing joy and fulfillment to the parent.

What about homeschools?

Although homeschools in this country have been around since the founding fathers, it was not until the late 1970s that the modern version came into flower. Because of the decline in public education—ignited, many believe, when God was expelled from the public school system by two infamous Supreme Court rulings in the early 1960s—a growing number of Christian families began to keep their children home and teach them around the kitchen table.

Operating largely in secret, until state legislatures finally softened their opposition, homeschools had to prove themselves to a skeptical audience. Now their value is widely acknowledged, albeit grudgingly in some quarters. Even traditional Christian schools still occasionally take a condescending view, despite the fact that homeschools have legally been out of the closet for years and have staked their claim on the educational landscape. At one point in their battle for respect, homeschools ironically became the darling of the American Civil Liberties Union, typically no friend of fundamental Christianity. Now the movement is firmly entrenched as an accepted alternative to the conventional school.

How, then, are conventional Christian schools to view homeschools? Is there room for fellowship, involvement? Or should we keep them at arm's length? Are homeschools competitors? Will they eventually put us out of business?

No need to worry. Most parents have neither the time nor the inclination to embark upon such an arrangement. And, no, homeschoolers are not typically affiliated with some militia group carrying on a vendetta with the IRS. They are rational, dedicated Christian folk who have taken the plunge only after much soul searching. They take the biblical mandate to "train up a child" personally, and some would contend that they follow the model of Deuteronomy 6 closer than we do.

The homeschool movement deserves our support, and there are many opportunities for involvement. Some conventional Christian schools have implemented a *satellite* arrangement with homeschools to monitor their curriculum and educational outcomes, to administer standardized tests, and to allow joint field trips and athletics.

Even if nothing this elaborate is ever birthed, simply taking a friendly posture toward homeschools can bring dividends. Conventional Christian schools that freely offer help and advice to homeschools often find themselves the beneficiaries when these same families later enroll their children.

It's all in your mind

Parent involvement begins with a school's mindset. If a school views parents more as antagonists than partners, more as an annoyance than allies, then nothing will come of the marriage.

Some of us fear allowing parents to be too involved in our schools, lest they "take over." We fear that soon they'll be lobbying the school board to remove the "ancient landmarks"; standards will be lowered and students will run amuck in the hallways! Understandably, since many of our parents are unsaved, such fears are not groundless. But the tendency is to retreat into our protective shells even when the threat is minimal. Hence, we come across to our public as secretive, clannish...with something to hide.

The Christian school, if it is to build a strong partnership, must keep such distrust in check. It is only when we assume a team approach, pooling our efforts for the common good of the children, that parents will find our school—and our Lord—attractive. An adversarial mentality has no place in the Christian school.

When we involve parents, we more often than not build strong bonds, and they end up being our most outspoken supporters. Not only that, but their own children benefit. Dozens of studies have concluded that the more involved parents are in their child's education, the better the child performs.

A common misconception among teachers and administrators is that parents resent being asked to be involved. They're busy, and we're imposing on their time. Although that is true in some instances—indeed, some parents pay their tuition, rarely set foot on campus, and that's the way they like it—the average parent wants to be involved. On the whole, according to Gallup and other pollsters, parents welcome opportunities for active participation. And private-school parents, because they have a financial investment at stake, are often especially eager to be an integral part of their child's education. In this respect, we are the envy of public-school educators.

Christian schools have discovered that parent bonding is often predicated upon their mindset, their viewpoint of parents as a whole. It is inextricably connected. When the welcome sign is out, bonds will form.

CHAPTER TEN

DEVELOPING A SPIRITUAL
RESTORATION PROGRAM

*"Its purpose was to balance the law of the school's code of
conduct with an avenue for restorative grace."*
—**Dan L. Burrell, Ed.D.**

The students would eventually refer to it as *Black Thursday*. Word had finally leaked to the administration about a party that had been held the previous weekend. Eight students from our Christian high school had been in attendance and the beverage-*du-jour* was the rage party drink of that time period—wine coolers. Of the eight in attendance, six had succumbed to the temptation and drank. Two had carried theirs around to appear "cool." Our school maintains a zero-tolerance policy of no use of alcohol. The penalty is immediate expulsion.

My job as the school administrator was to unearth the facts and administer the penalties. I went to our pastor and told him of the problem. Together we prayed for wisdom and discernment. For hours, the appointments were scheduled for interviews in the conference room. Parents were called. Confessions poured out. A lot of us cried. The rules were clear; expulsions were to follow. We grieved for those who had fallen. We had to protect the integrity of the code of conduct. Our hearts were breaking as long-time students from outstanding families cleaned out their lockers.

Not every student was repentant. Some hurled accusations of inconsistency; others dropped into a steely silence. But several were shaken to the core, shoulders quaking with gut-wrenching sobs. Red-eyed parents looked longingly at us for some signal that this was all some sort of mistake or that we'd let it "pass" just this once.

Sleep did not come easily that night. The next day most of us just went through the motions. In a high school with fewer than 150 students, the loss of six of the most well-known was felt in virtually every classroom. Some were angry with their friends who had been so foolish and weak. Others were angry at what they perceived to be a graceless system of rules and regulations that refused to take into account the pressures and temptations of adolescence. In my heart, I was torn. I loved those kids. I was a close personal friend with some of their parents. But I also knew that if a line was not drawn and respected, a floodgate would be opened, and alcohol and drug use and other serious offenses would never be viewed as *serious* again.

Then one of the students who had been expelled made an appointment with me. Trembling, this attractive and intelligent young lady brought her parents into my office. Softly first, the words came out one by one and then with a voice that gained strength, the trickle became a torrent. "It was wrong. I've destroyed my reputation. I have no excuse. This school is my life. If I go back to the public school, I'll never survive the pressure. My parents don't deserve this. Is there *anyway* that I can become a student in this school again?" And then she fell silent.

There was an uncomfortable silence broken only by the sound of a typewriter in an adjoining office. The girl's father wiped his red-rimmed eyes for the thousandth time in the last forty-eight hours. His wife twisted her handkerchief into an even-tighter knot. In my heart, I knew that Christ would have found a way to administer grace to this girl.

Within a couple of days, a plan was formulated and approved by our school board and church deacons. We called it the Spiritual Restoration Plan. Its purpose was to balance the *law* of the school's code of conduct with an avenue for restorative grace. It was crafted in such a way that it would not be perceived as being *soft* on sin, but did provide a way to be restored into the student body.

The Scriptures support the concept of a process for spiritual restoration. Matthew 18 and Galatians 6 are two obvious examples of how restoration can be undertaken and what the goal of spiritual restoration should be. It is sometimes easier and more convenient to adopt a rigid mentality that disposes of unseemly problems. And sometimes, the expulsion of a few rebellious students will do much to improve the atmosphere and morale of a class or school. At the same time, most experienced educators can think of an occasion when a good student simply made a poor choice and succumbed to sin. Their heart is broken, their repentance is genuine, and it is my opinion that God expects us to respond according to the example of Christ and become agents of His grace.

The following is a list of some of the principles that were used in formulating this policy. From this list of principles, you may be able to forge your own restoration program. A sample policy is also included near the end of this chapter. You should understand that no policy is 100 percent successful, and there is a maintenance price you must be willing to pay in order to make the policy work. But I am convinced that the potential for restoration will make the difference in the lives of some who genuinely made a grievous error in judgment and who will flourish under the grace of a second chance.

The student must initiate the plan

It was our opinion that in order for the program to be effective, it had to be the desire of the *student*. Many of us have seen the wayward child of a prominent church member get into trouble and then have had to experience the pressure that comes from Mom and Dad for Junior to be given some "slack." As the young rebel glowers at you from beneath a scowling brow, you wonder to yourself why the well-intentioned parent does not see that the child's presence in a Christian school is not likely to change the heart problem that exists.

If the student has not truly repented and does not express a personal desire to be restored, there is little chance that changed behavior will be observed. It is possible for coerced kids who enter into your office under the threatening cloud of their displeased parents to give some lip service about wanting to *come back* to the school, but an experienced and discerning educator will quickly be able to ascertain the genuineness of the appeal. It becomes important that the administrator maintains a sufficiently strong will to wait until genuine brokenness has occurred, and then and only then can authentic restoration take place.

There have been several occasions when an insincere student, who was merely doing the bidding of the parents, was denied entry into the restoration program. After time passed, the student might have become genuinely convicted of his or her sin—while attending a church or youth service or upon a harsh dose of the *real* world in one of our local mega-public high schools—that he returned to seek reconsideration once again with a far different attitude. It was when a genuine demonstration of repentance at the initiative of the student in crisis occurred that real progress was made.

There must be a request to a board

In our school, not every expulsion is approved by our board. If it is in a gray area, the board reviews it; but in those areas where the policy and the infraction are very clear, the board does not ask to review the decision. However, the board hears appeals to expulsion. This provides a measure of protection and accountability for the administration. The pressure upon the administrator to give the child of a prominent family a second chance can be quite substantial. By using a governing board as a part of the appeals process, it provides safety and a system of checks and balances.

A letter from the student is required, and the option of having the student appear before the board is also reserved. There should be a measure of inconvenience and discomfort in this process to validate its integrity. If it is a cakewalk, then students observing from the mainstream of your school may assume that the school is *easy* on offenses on which their policy claims to be tough.

There must be local church involvement

Because our school is a ministry of a local church, this is convenient for us. In the vast majority of the cases, we require the student to attend our church a minimum of two services per week for a set period of time. We make very few exceptions to this policy. By having them attend our church, we know the message that they are receiving, we can verify that they are attending and, hopefully, a pattern will be established which will continue beyond the terms of the restoration period.

On extremely rare occasions, if the student is active in a sound Bible-preaching church in which we have confidence and have regular conversations with the pastor or youth leaders, we will allow a student to attend another church. It is our expectation that the leadership of that church would undertake a role in the spiritual growth and restoration of the student and work with us in this spiritual mission.

A mentoring relationship must be established

We feel that the existence of a spiritual mentor is key to the success of the spiritual restoration program. The individual who works with the student in this capacity can be the single most effective factor in the process. There are several facets to the mentor's responsibility.

1.   **Accountability:** We require that there be a regular meeting held no less than once each week between the student and the mentor. The mentor must let the administration know if the student fails to attend their sessions.

2.   **Discipleship:** There should be a weekly lesson that centers on the Scriptures and has a practical application of a biblical principle. We also encourage the memorization of the Scriptures, though we do not want the memory assignments to appear to be *punishment* for the infraction, but a natural part of the discipleship process. We are philosophically opposed to using the Bible as a tool for punishment.

3. **Relationship:** We hope that a relationship between the student and the mentor will be created that will endure well past the time required by the program. Research indicates that the primary reason good kids get into trouble is because of the influence of a friend. We believe that this can work in the opposite as well. If a good relationship is established during the program and continues after the restoration, the influence of the mentor over the long-term may prevent a relapse and may lead to a spiritually enriching relationship which will be a blessing to both individuals for many years.

4. **Advocacy:** The mentor will become an advocate for (and occasionally against) the student. He or she will have to give a report as to the student's progress and their recommendation for re-admittance is required. In addition, they may suggest modifications to the program, extensions and exceptions.

When selecting a mentor, it should be done with sufficient care that will ensure that there is a certain "chemistry" between the student and the mentor. There must be a substantial level of maturity on the part of the mentor, and the commitment required of the mentor should be clearly explained. In the past, we have used teachers, youth directors, lay people, Sunday school teachers, deacons, senior citizens and a wide variety of mentors to fulfill this vital role.

There must be substantial ramifications for the offense

Acceptance into the restoration program provides for a way to re-enter our school but does not mean that there is no "sting" to the punishment. In order to ensure that the student and those that observe how the infraction was handled realize the seriousness of an offense that leads to expulsion, we use most, if not all, of the following penalties:

1. **Time out of class:** Depending on the infraction and upon acceptance into the restoration program, we may *suspend* an expulsion (if the student does not complete the program, the expulsion is noted on the cumulative folder). In place of the expulsion, we require a suspension that can be from one week to one semester in duration. Generally, it is either one week, ten days or a semester, depending on the reason for expulsion. If it is likely that the student will return after the suspension and a parent will be at home to home-school the student, then the work may be laid out for completion. This works best for one- or two-week suspensions but has been done with limited success for as long as a semester. Careful monitoring is necessary, of course.

2. **Loss of privilege:** Generally, the student may not participate in extracurricular activities for one semester after returning to class. This allows the student to reflect on the gravity of his or her offense and to focus on the academic areas. This is often the most painful part of the restoration process.

3. **Reconciliation:** Upon or prior to the student's return to school, the student must reconcile with those whom he or she has offended. This can be in the form of written or oral apologies and should be part of the discipleship process under the tutelage of the mentor. It is sometimes necessary to extend apologies to the administration, faculty, the stu-

dent body, individual students, the parents of another student or others. This is biblical (Matthew 5:23–24) and again provides a good example as to how genuine restoration and reconciliation should take place.

The Presence of Grace

It is very important that the Spiritual Restoration Plan not be turned into a legalistic *program*, whereby a student with the fortitude to endure a series of hoops through which he must jump is rewarded by gaining re-admission into the school. The spirit of the administration and the design of the program must be firm, but loving. The student should be able to sense the resolve and the eagerness of the administration in seeing that the student is biblically restored. There should be affirmation as the student does right, and there should be an insistence that the process be complete and thorough. This balance is essential to the success of the plan.

There can be a wide variety of plans designed and you will want to develop more than one. A plan may look like this when it is completed:

- **Infraction:** Consumption of alcohol.
- **Policy Response:** Expulsion.
- **Restoration Plan:**

  a) Student will attend First Church at least two services each week and shall attend the youth activities as scheduled.
  b) Student will meet weekly for a minimum of 16 weeks with the youth director of First Church for a time of devotion, Bible study and Bible application.

161

c) Student will volunteer for a community service for 20 hours during a 2-week suspension.

d) Student will not be permitted to participate in extra-curricular activities for one semester.

e) Student will maintain a 3.0 GPA to receive no detention time for at least one semester.

f) Student will reconcile with his class via an apology to be delivered during homeroom. (This requirement may best be left as part of the discipleship objectives, and it may not be wise to announce this as a *requirement*; rather, have it be viewed as *evidence* of genuine spiritual growth.)

g) Student understands that failure to abide by the plan or committing any future major violation will result in expulsion. (It has been our experience that one opportunity at a restoration plan is all that really works.)

Again, let me emphasize that how you develop the restoration plan should be the result of prayer, counseling and discernment. The list above is a cold instrument. The power of a compassionate heart and a loving voice is what will make the difference. "And of some, have compassion, making a difference" (Jude 22).

The girl that I mentioned at the onset of this chapter? She is now married to a fine young man and they have two children. She teaches Sunday school. They rarely miss a church service. She is a mentor to a troubled young lady. Every time that I look at her, I see a beautiful monument to God's grace and the joy of genuine personal ministry. To quote Paul Harvey: "And now you know the *rest* of the story."

THE AUTHORS

Dan L. Burrell, Ed.D., Author

Dr. Burrell is the senior pastor of Berean Baptist Church and superintendent of Berean Christian Schools in West Palm Beach, Florida. He has served as a junior and senior high schoolteacher, a school administrator and is the president of the Florida Association of Christian Colleges and Schools. Dr. Burrell holds a master's degree in educational administration from Pensacola Christian College and a doctorate in educational administration from Nova Southeastern University. He and his wife, Julie, have 4 children. Dr. Burrell is known for straight talk and practical ideas. Look for thought-provoking commentary and suggestions for implementation in his chapters.

Philip C. Johnson, Ph.D., Editor and Author

Dr. Johnson is the Director of Educational Services for the Florida Association of Christian Colleges and Schools. He earned his master's degree in education at Pensacola Christian College and a Ph.D. at Andrew Jackson University in Birmingham. He served as a classroom teacher and school administrator before assuming his current position. He is a frequent conference speaker and author. He and his wife, Haeryeon, have two sons, Kris and Sam. Dr. Johnson's unique blend of heart, humor and disciplined thinking will make his chapters a joy to read and a blessing to implement.

Paul Tatham, M.S., Author

Paul Tatham has a master of science degree in educational administration from Bob Jones University. He and his wife, Susie, have three daughters, all of whom spent their entire elementary and secondary education at The King's Academy in West Palm Beach, where Paul has served as a teacher and dean of academics since 1972. Prior to that, Paul was an administrator of Kingsway Academy in the Bahamas and Tulsa Christian Academy in Oklahoma. He has written extensively in various Christian publications and has been involved with several Christian school associations.

To order additional copies of

Perspectives In Christian Education

Focus On Parent & Student Relationships

please send $12.99*
plus $4.50 shipping and handling to:

FACCS Office of Educational Services
PO Box 210727
West Palm Beach, FL 33421

*Quantity Discounts Available